The Eyes of

G000254330

After some years with the Overseas Missionary Fellowship in Thailand, the Revd Dennis Lennon was ordained into the Church of England. He served at the Round Church, and then at St Barnabas, both in Cambridge. From St Thomas Episcopal Church in Edinburgh, notable for its church planting experiments, he moved to Shef-field to become Diocesan Adviser in Evangelism. Dennis is married and has two children.

For Soni –
great looker, lovely listener

The Eyes of the Heart

A spirituality of the senses

DENNIS LENNON

TRIANGLE

First published in Great Britain in 2000 by
Triangle, SPCK,
Holy Trinity Church,
Marylebone Road, London NW1 4DU

© Dennis Lennon 2000

All rights reserved. No part of this book may be reproduced or
transmitted in any form or by any means, electronic or
mechanical, including photocopying, recording, or by any
information storage and retrieval system, without permission
in writing from the publisher.

ACKNOWLEDGEMENTS
Unless otherwise stated, biblical quotations are from
the New International Version, copyright © 1973, 1978, 1984 by
the International Bible Society. Published by Hodder & Stoughton.

British Library Cataloguing-in-Publication Data

A catalogue record for this book is available from
The British Library

ISBN 0-281-05296-4

Typeset by Pioneer Associates, Perthshire
Printed in Great Britain by
Omnia Books Ltd, Glasgow

Contents

CHAPTER 1

Beyond the web

An anthropologist asked an old Hopi woman why Hopi songs are so short. 'Our songs are short', she replied, 'because we all know so much.' By that reckoning you may feel that this small book about looking and listening need be only a very small book indeed. First, because 'we all know so much' about the subject already, having used our eyes and ears quite successfully all our lives. And second, because we are in the time of the almighty IT revolution.

What is a revolution in communications for if not to extend and empower our abilities to see and hear? And this current revolution is not coy about its claims to do just that. Indeed, its self-confidence is breathtaking (it's 'the greatest advance in human society since the discovery of fire', according to one blurb), implicitly claiming an omnipresence and an omniscience which Christians previously believed to be the property of the Holy Spirit! 'How many Microsoft engineers does it take to change a light bulb? None – Bill Gates will simply redefine light.'

But on the ground things are not working out as smoothly as those remarks imply. Not once we introduce into the equation the realities of soft-skinned, warm-blooded, feeling, longing, vulnerable, hopeful, anxious human beings. The word 'communication' contains a hint of two other words, 'communion' and 'community', rich words signalling our spiritual aspirations.

It is quite clear that something very odd is going on among us. We live in a strange contradiction whereby quite astonishing systems of inter-personal communication thrive alongside extensive isolation and loneliness, like hungry people in the midst of a food-glut. So much communication, so little communion.

Ironic that in our 'information-driven' society with its 'knowledge-rich' economy, real looking and listening between people (as in communion and community) should be so elusive. At a time when just about anyone can 'access' just about anyone else, the social indicators of personal isolation are rising alarmingly: depression, stress, marital breakdown, personal alienation, family disintegration, single-occupation accommodation, addiction and suicide (particularly in the 16–19 age range) are some of the more obvious signs. Less obvious statistically, but just as real, is the widely shared perception that more and more of our national life is slipping towards superficiality and artificiality, especially in the ways we encounter and respond to one another in daily life. The old courtesies are too time-consuming; they are giving way to quicker, more superficial contact. 'There's something ails our colt' and it's bound up with the business of looking and listening.

Once in the *New York Times*, 'A health director [. . .] reported this week that a small mouse, which presumably has been watching television, attacked a little girl and her full-grown cat [. . .] both mouse and cat survived, and the incident is recorded here as a reminder that things seem to be changing.'[1] Indeed they are and we can chance a guess at what is driving the trend. Unlike the Hopi granny and her people who shared an agreed understanding of life and its main mysteries, ours is the individualist and fragmented world of modernity. The historian Toynbee has said that out of twenty civilizations in world history this one of ours is the first which has no agreed understanding of what the meaning of life is. An atomized world-view generates an atomized society in which the looking and listening which enact communion and community between us are early casualties.

More and more of us find we have less and less need, or opportunity, to spend time with others. Consider our patterns of eating, which is done mostly alone. We are mobile and wired, connected to others but effectively out of communion with them. Our mutual encounters tend to be ephemeral, open-ended, unrooted; we avoid the word or glance which might engage us more deeply with others.

By now it is clear that the approach of this book assumes looking and listening to be spiritual activities as much as physical ones. Therefore we must take note of certain attitudes which filter out our powers of observation and subvert our willingness to look and listen at depth. For now we mention just two. No doubt self-worship has always been the essence of sin and therefore a malign force in human relationships, destructive of communion and community. It is as old as Eden. But no other age has justified narcissism so enthusiastically and been so breathtakingly blunt in embracing the celebration of the self as the highest good. Such a person fills his own horizons, he casts his own thick shadow across everything he looks at. Indeed, he cannot see because he is not sufficiently free from himself to see.

A second factor distorting our sight and hearing is a pervasive secular scepticism in our culture. Its effects are dramatically illustrated by the report that Balinese temple dancers, who from their earliest years are trained to enter the trance-like state of mind in which their gestures and movements can happen, completely lose the ability after even a short exposure to Western attitudes. We experience the same process in our own society through a stealthy osmosis which colonizes our inner world and drains our spiritual powers of discernment. The music is playing but we cannot hear it.

We are not seriously proposing to blame the Internet, fax or their various offspring for this state of affairs. For now, we simply want to make the point that 'communication' as celebrated across our society is clearly unable to produce a quality and reality of looking and listening between people which is fundamental to our humanity. The technologies are awesomely clever and are able to deliver enormous benefits, but they have their dark side also, they can mesmerize the unwary like the juicy piece of meat offered by the burglar to distract the guard dog of the mind. Their power and brilliance prevent us from noticing what is missing: they lack wisdom. We swim in rivers of information, news, data, pictures, knowledge, but where is the wisdom?

In the Bible 'wisdom' means understanding, and especially the skills to make understanding issue in appropriate action. It is, in biblical thought, practical rather than theoretical and philosophical. 'Wisdom' understands what it is that makes things tick. It is grounded in the belief that God is the creator of every existing thing; and therefore everything has meaning and purpose, it is governed by an order, with rhyme and reason and with laws and principles which protect it and release it to run joyously. 'How many are your works, O Lord! In wisdom you made them all' (Psalm 104.24).

The wise God not only designs and creates wisely but actually imprints 'wisdom' into the texture of creation as an attribute. Everything receives its own truth from God as a gift; 'wisdom' consists in seeking to understand the truth of things, and honouring that truth in the way we handle it and respond to it. 'Great are the works of the Lord; they are pondered by all who delight in them' (Psalm 111.2) suggests an approach of openness to and respect for the wisdom of God in creation. We ponder creation properly (look at it, listen to it) when we turn to the Lord as the One who holds all life in his hands.

Wisdom is first and last God's wisdom in which he invites us to participate. Hence the fundamental principle for the art of looking and listening is always: 'The fear of the Lord is the beginning of wisdom, and knowledge of the Holy One is understanding' (Proverbs 9.10).

This basic truth is cast into a very wonderful poem in Job chapter 28. People know (feel, intuit, take it as self-evident) that wisdom is 'there' in the world somewhere and that life cannot be lived without it. But where? They mine deep into the earth in the not unreasonable idea that priceless wisdom will be found near to precious stones and metals. But no. Wisdom (the truth and the practical purpose of things) cannot be found in separation from God. 'Only a rumour of it has reached our ears,' say destruction and death. 'God understands the way to it and he alone knows where it dwells' (Job 28.22, 23). Therefore the person learning to look and listen in the world will be a worshipping man or woman, one who 'fears' (not the same as being afraid of), adores and respects God as the source and fountain of wisdom for all life. Kepler, the great astronomer, spoke of the seventeenth-century scientists of genius who launched the scientific age as 'priests officiating around the altar of the creator'. And Newton was delighted when others found his work to be a storehouse of pointers towards the maker and creator of all things. Those great investigators thought that scientific work was, in Boyle's words, a means to the 'seraphic love' of God. They acknowledged that wisdom is found in the fear of the Lord.

Our capacity for perception is as much God's gift, along with his gifts to us of eyes and ears, as the world we perceive. There is a wisdom governing our minds, our looking and listening, and a corresponding wisdom governing the world we observe. The one key to both is with God. Therefore, along with practical reverence for God, we need also humility. Humility is wisdom's inseparable twin (Proverbs 18.12). Humility before the Lord who exclusively bestows powers of perception to see and hear at the heart of things. And humility before the world teeming around us, an attitude of curiosity, respect and teachableness which allows God to disclose what he wants us to discern.

It follows that pride and arrogance are self-binding attitudes. The blight of prevailing secularism is that quite unconsciously we conform to plausible attitudes of false self-sufficiency and autonomy. But how deadening and limiting their effect is upon us. And how emancipating and expanding it is to realize and embrace that we, and the wisdom by which to interpret life, are God's gifts: 'Everything is gift; the receiver of the gift is himself the first gift received.'[2]

Now we can move on with our exploration of looking and listening, by first looking into the mirror.

CHAPTER 2

Facing out

Ե Ե Ե

Arranged in and around the face are our chief means of detecting and perceiving the world, our eyes and ears. We have other means also, of course, for each of the senses plays its part in the teeming exchange of messages between ourselves and the world. One family doctor claims that he sometimes is able to smell disease; 'I can smell domestic disquiet; I can smell unhappiness', which is a thoroughly Christian use of the nose! Believers in the past valued the sacredness of the senses, referring to them as 'talismans of the Lord', each one gifted to take some part in the mystery of creation. Obviously our greatest powers of perception are our sight and hearing.

Two spheres, the eyes, are the gateways for light from a friend's face to enter the nerve-wiring pathways to the brain where it is processed into the image of her face. Our ears, these rather comic-looking scoops set like jug handles on either side of the head, funnel the vibrations of our friend's voice along the labyrinth towards the brain where they are decoded as her distinctive voice. But sight is more than a camera, and hearing is more than a voice-detector. Looking towards that friend while at the same time hearing her voice stirs and engages our inner world. The images and sounds undergo mysterious transformations in the brain as they are permeated with many emotions – memories, imagination, a history, happiness or perhaps sadness, curiosity, hope – all synchronized into a unified whole. By their seemingly magical interplay and exchange we find ourselves visualizing the words we hear, and putting into words the images we see.

A chilling moment at school was the rebuke 'Look at me boy when I'm talking to you!' Why does the teacher need to see my face? He cannot have forgotten what it looks like; two ears, two eyes, a mouth, a nose, like most of the other children there. Why cannot he be satisfied with a view of the back of my head, or my left knee, all parts which are no less me? Because when we 'face' another person we turn towards him our essential selves, the sign of our personality, our best means of paying attention, observation, perception. To 'face' someone is a universal gesture of courtesy and sincerity.

And it shows. The play of expressions, of thoughts reflected in the features of the face, pale or blushing, can communicate as effectively and sometimes more truthfully than words. 'It's written all over your face.' Eyes are proverbially the windows of the soul, which is why in some Far Eastern societies it is a discourtesy, as well as arousing suspicion, to wear sunglasses while in conversation. And eyes can 'drink in' a sunrise. Shakespeare would even have us believe that not only can eyes speak, they can also listen: 'to hear with eyes belongs to love's fine wit' (Sonnet 23). Perhaps that is why inscrutable people make us uneasy. On the other hand babies learn to smile by being smiled at; they are smiled into smiling. Such is the uncanny power of the face.

This ability to give attention in more than one way may explain why in the Hebrew of the Old Testament the word for face is in the plural, *panim*. And one further thing about the face, and it's the most obvious of all: our eyes face outwards. They are not turned inwards, Buddha-like, gazing towards our own inner centre. Nor are our ears inverted to catch sounds coming from our own centre. They are directed outwards towards the external world. We are designed to be outward facing, outward living people, facing the oncoming world, finding our life and fulfilment through interplay with creation and history.

Therefore an evocative image of our communion with God

is that of looking at the face which is looking at us. The ancient Aaronic blessing articulates the deepest longings of the human heart, the experience we were created for and without which we would be doomed to frustration '... The Lord make his face shine upon you and be gracious to you; the Lord turn his face towards you and give you peace' (Numbers 6.25–6). The face of God suggests his intimate nearness and his incomprehensible distance. Jewish poets have celebrated the unbearable glories of the divine countenance:

> Lovely face, majestic face, face of beauty, face of flame[...] Whoever looks at Him is instantly torn; whoever glimpses his beauty immediately melts away. Those who serve him [...] their strength fails and their faces are charred, their heads reel and their eyes grow dim at the splendour and radiance of their king's beauty [...] Happy the eye that sees and feeds upon this wondrous light – a wondrous vision and most strange![1]

Desires that were taken up and fulfilled with astonishing literalism (beyond anything Aaron's priests dared to imagine) in the face of the man, Jesus Christ: God 'made his light shine in our hearts to give us the light of the knowledge of the glory of God in the face of Christ' (2 Corinthians 4.6).

Because God in Christ turned his face towards us (seen in our hearts, says the apostle Paul, by the power of the Holy Spirit) we know we have all his love and his full attention with all his powers of looking and listening. What an astonishing encouragement for faith and prayer this is!

Stay with the physical literalism of Christ's face. Everything we said about our own face is equally true of his. Arranged in and around his face were his chief powers of detecting and perceiving the world he came to save, his eyes and ears. The nerve-pathways from eyes and ears to his brain were the same as ours. When a speck of dust from a Nazareth street lodged in his eye it irritated and threatened infection, just as with any other person there. When water got into his ears whilst swimming in Lake Galilee it temporarily deafened him, as it would any other swimmer. It is an uncanny thought that the creator and redeemer of the world limited himself to life within our human powers of sight and hearing. 'Since the children have flesh and blood, he too shared in their humanity' (Hebrews 2.14). It had to be that way because he came to save us in the totality of our real, human, bodily life, including our looking and our listening.

But when we turn to Christ's teaching on the use of our eyes and ears, we are struck by the absence of instruction on 'how to'. We find nothing on methods or techniques. Yet we know from practical experience that exercises and techniques can be useful in improving our powers of concentration, memory, and detailed observation. But we find none of it in Jesus' teaching. Rather, he seems wholly concerned with the quality of inner life of the person who is doing the looking and listening. Apparently, the sort of person you are determines how well you see and hear.

Incidentally, Jesus treated speech by the same principle. Do you want to be a 'good' speaker whose words convey blessing to other people? Jesus said: 'The good man brings good things out of the good stored up in his heart, and the evil man brings evil things out of the evil stored up in his heart. For out of the overflow of his heart his mouth speaks' (Luke 6.45). Good speech requires not elocution lessons but personal holiness and an inner climate in which good things can flourish. '. . . [W]hatever is true, whatever is noble, whatever is right, whatever is pure, whatever is lovely, whatever is admirable – if anything is excellent or praiseworthy – think about such things' (Philippians 4.8). Such thought will spill out into the words you speak and it will profoundly affect the way you look at and perceive the world.

Jesus was interested in the eye of the beholder on the grounds that we are able to see only what our eyes allow us to see. Who will see God? The pure in heart (Matthew 5.8). Not because the sight of God is granted as a reward for personal purity, but because the pure heart is, like a clean window, transparent.

Jesus described that person as truth-loving and light-seeking, one who turns towards God's face as a compass needle seeks magnetic north. That person continuously, habitually, brings his thoughts, imagination, plans and behaviour 'into the light, so that it may be seen plainly that what he has done has been done through God' (John 3.21).

As a boy of ten, William Blake was out walking one day on Peckham Rye in London. He writes that he saw a vision, a tree filled with angels whose 'bright angelic wings bespangled every bough like stars'. At home he related his experience to his family and only the intervention of his mother saved him from a thrashing by his father 'for lying'. Years later Blake coined the proverb, 'a fool sees not the same tree that a wise man sees!' And, right in line with Jesus' teaching, he arrived at the principle of right looking and wise observation: 'As the man is so he sees; as the eye is formed such are its powers.' Hence the quaint yet profound aphorism from the ancient church that 'the eye can see the sun because the eye is the same shape as the sun'.

Jesus also said, 'Your eye is the lamp of your body. When your eyes are good, your whole body also is full of light. But when they are bad, your body also is full of darkness. See to it, then, that the light within you is not darkness. Therefore, if your whole body is full of light, and no part of it dark, it will be completely lighted, as when the light of a lamp shines on you' (Luke 11.34–6). Ancient physiology understood the eye to be 'the lamp of your body' because it stands like a transparent window on the boundary between the outer and the inner worlds. A good eye is one which is free from cataracts or other disorders; it is sound, healthy and like a clean window allows in the light which irradiates the inner world of that person.

Indeed, Jesus went further in suggesting that the illuminated inner personality becomes as it were incandescent ('completely lighted, as when the light of a lamp shines on you') – that is, the outer body, the face and skin, glows and gives off light, it becomes a source of illumination in the darkness. In that situation it is possible to see what is there waiting to be seen. But everything depends upon the state of the eyes.

The 'good eye' of Christ's teaching, like the pure heart, means spiritually healthy, sincere, simple, single, transparent, having no trace of duplicity, hypocrisy or double-dealing in one's relationship with God or with others. It is another image of the light- and truth-loving person whose first instinct is to seek God's good pleasure in all of life. That person can see.

And there is a further fascinating slant to the word translated 'good', and that is 'generous'. The 'generous eye' reflects God, it is a Christ-like attitude. The generous attitude has the effect in our lives of clearing and healing our eyesight. Conversely the 'bad' or 'evil' eye carried the idea of mean, grudging, critical, tight-fisted and judgemental attitudes which have the effect of being self-blinding.

In other words, believing precedes seeing, and makes seeing possible. A believing and encouraging attitude towards others (and nothing is more encouraging than to be believed) creates a local climate of respect and trust. Suspicion and its close relative cynicism give way to transparency. The generous eye invites the other person to come through and make herself known. Thus we are able to 'see' that person.

Conversely, you may have been on the receiving end of 'bad' eye attitudes. Perhaps at an interview or in a discussion, you came away knowing that you were unable, as we say, to 'get through' to the other person. It was, as we say in a telling image, 'like knocking my head against a brick wall'. You encountered a cool suspicion, they were unwilling to give you a fair chance to present yourself, or allow you the benefit of the doubt, their minds were already made up about you (where 'made up' means not the Liverpudlian idiom 'happy for you' but its opposite, 'closed against you'). Because they were not prepared to approach you with a generous, believing slant of mind (a creative bias), their grudging, tight-lipped attitude lowered the shutters (a destructive bias). There was no disclosure, no seeing, because there was no believing.

If that has been your experience you are in the best company possible. Our Lord Jesus himself could not penetrate Jewish bias or perform his miracles, because of unbelief (Matthew 13.58). Believing precedes seeing.

But the generous mind, although it does risk exploitation by others and is apparently naïve and too trusting, allows the reality of the other person to come through. Perhaps it is this idea of the generous eye which helps to account for the Bible's preoccupation with the way we use our money and resources. It is typical of scripture that it will not allow us to falsely over-spiritualize the idea of the 'good' eye. Healthy eyesight is linked to practical open-handedness. One out of every seven verses in the New Testament deals with the use of money. Altogether scripture offers about fifty verses on prayer, and fewer than fifty on faith, while there are more than two thousand verses on money. Austin Farrer goes so far as to suggest that 'what we have done with our money is what we have done with our life. The man who has made an imaginative, a generous, a just, a creative, a living use of his money is a perfect man.'[2] He has a good eye. He can see.

CHAPTER 3

Piercing illusions

It is the strangest thing about everyday life that the longer we know people or things, the less we 'see' them. What we see instead is the greatest illusion of all – the illusion of familiarity. We spend most of our time in the realm of the familiar and on the whole we are glad for it. A framework of the habitual and routine helps to keep life sane and manageable. But at a price. The illusion induced by familiarity (or the lethargy of imagination that familiarity creates) is fatal to wonder, awe, surprise, expectation and hope. It distorts and diminishes everything it touches.

By definition, unusual or startling events are beyond the reach of familiarity. Cruising down the Java coast while Krakatoa is erupting we need no one to call our attention to the spectacle of a lifetime. Unfortunately for us our normal Monday mornings fall some way short of that level of exotica. Tuesday and even Wednesday mornings are little better and there lies the challenge to our sight and hearing: how do we get on with the ordinary, the unexciting, the boringly well-known? 'Our perennial spiritual and psychological task is to look at things familiar until they become unfamiliar again,' said that penetrating observer of life, G. K. Chesterton.

A first step in following Chesterton's advice, in de-illusioning our sight and hearing from the effects of familiarity, will be to probe the origins of the problem. That is easier said than done. Illusion, like seduction, creeps over the unsuspecting mind unawares. We seldom catch it happening, but we must try.

14

Most obviously *neglect* is a chief culprit in the process of illusion. Familiarity breeds neglect on its way, famously, to breeding contempt. When a marriage is failing expect signs of steady, gradual, unthinking neglect. A man grows bored with his marriage and soon he no longer 'sees' his wife for the person she is. Or a more entertaining instance of costly neglect is found in the hugely popular TV programme *The Antiques Roadshow* with its many delicious moments of disclosure as old objects are brought out of the shadows of familiarity for re-evaluation. So we watch as a woman produces a large vase for the expert to examine. She explains that the vase has served as her family's umbrella stand since the Boer War. But we can see that the man from Sotheby's is not hearing her, he is absorbed in the vase, he is excited, even elated. Then comes the stunning revelation: the old 'umbrella stand' was in fact Ghengis Khan's Ming spittoon and absolutely priceless.

At that moment around the land viewers are glancing at their various bits and pieces with new eyes. We say with 'new eyes'. What is wrong with their usual 'old' eyes which have served pretty well for so long? They are hopelessly conditioned and misfocused by years of casual, neglectful, familiarity with their personal world.

For 'Ming spittoon' perhaps we may read family, friends, neighbours, church, locality, and the wider circle of acquaintances and colleagues. Perhaps we are, dare we say, mistaking a Ming vase for an umbrella stand? People you know so well (or so you assume) that you have long since ceased to look for, or expect, any fresh thing to emerge from them. In your scheme of things, the way you arrange your inner world of value and importance, you have those individuals weighed, measured, labelled, and placed. Not with deliberate cynical intention of course but simply by losing them in the foggy processes of familiarity and neglect. Neglect of the idea that those folk might yet possess unimagined depths and potential. And, even more reprehensible, total neglect of the possibility that God the Holy Spirit could be moving in those well-known lives. Neglect is the failure of imagination and hope. And of love: 'Love [. . .] always trusts, always hopes, always perseveres. Love never fails' (1 Corinthians 13.6, 7, 8). Love, we might add, always looks and listens.

But one thing love cannot do is to pretend. It will not look at people with starry-eyed unreal sentimentality which regards all geese as swans. No, the way in which we will be able to 'look at things familiar until they become unfamiliar again' is to do as that woman did with her vase when she took it along to the expert valuer. If we are serious about penetrating our routine personal world, to see and hear what is actually there, or even potentially there, then we must bring it all to God. Its real value and meaning is what God says it to be. Any description of reality less than that will only leave us on the outside of things and people.

Bring, for example, that neighbour of yours to God for evaluation. Allow God to tell you what to look for in that person. He is a man you see frequently, so how do you 'see' him? The usual way in which our society 'sees' people is in terms of the jobs they do and the roles they fulfil. Who is that man you know as your neighbour? You reply, he is a Scot, married, the father of two children, an engineer, a keen gardener and a supporter of Glasgow Rangers. But all you have done there is to list the roles and functions he fulfils. Who is this man? If he is promoted in his job and changes his car for a more prestigious model society looks at him and judges that 'he has gone up in the world'. That is, he is fulfilling certain of his roles more successfully than before. But should things go badly for him then he is reckoned to have 'gone down in the world'. By that reckoning you are what you have. A secularized culture really has no other yardstick by which to 'see' an individual. Meanwhile, inside the head of your neighbour, he knows, as his deepest instinct, that he is very much more than the sum-total of his jobs and roles. He has innate value and purpose in himself, but for the life of him he cannot put it into convincing words. So, who or what is he? Only God knows.

Regardless of your neighbour's thoughts on spiritual life, faith and religion (or the lack of them: he might be a paid-up member of the National Secular Society), God has spoken about the man's fundamental worth. Scripture is adamant in its teaching that he is inextricably involved with God in whom he 'lives and moves and has his being' (Acts 17.28). He might one day decide, as we say, to 'invite God into his life', and we understand what that phrase is trying to say. But at a more profound level he is God's guest. God was there first in the man's life before it existed, and welcomed him into life. At the very ground of his being your neighbour stands before his God and creator. It is this human nature of ours and our being that are God's guest. Nicholas of Cusa expressed the mysterious value and meaning of our being and our nature in its relationship with God in his prayer, 'How could you give yourself to me if you had not first given me to myself?' Life begins the moment I see my own existence as giftedness. The goal of the first gift is to make possible the second gift, namely, Christ in us.

Thus, without knowing anything about your neighbour, you know the most important thing about him: the mysterious worth of his being. And this you have not by analysis or investigation but by revelation. Bring him into focus, read him aright, by looking at him through the lens of God's word. And there is more.

At the incarnation of Jesus Christ God took on our human nature, lived within it as one of us, and died on the cross in our place and for our salvation. Then he rose from the dead, taking our bodily human nature into transformed, glorious, resurrection life in eternity. This event has fixed for ever the price-tag on each individual. Now you look at that neighbour of yours as 'your brother for whom Christ died' (Romans 14.15), even though as yet he neither knows it nor believes it.

He has the right to say, if he will, that Jesus is the Son of God 'who loved me and gave himself for me' (Galatians 2.20).

It is surely quite impossible to believe in Jesus as God become man and at the same time go through life ignoring the people around us in neglectful familiarity. The incarnation transforms the way we look at the whole sweep of ordinary life. It is a mystifying fact that Jesus spent the first thirty years of his life, before launching into his three-year public ministry, in virtual anonymity. God enters the human race through the miracle of the incarnation in order to redeem humankind – but spends most of the time in the humdrum small-village life of ancient Palestine. What was he doing for those thirty silent years? Entering, living, embracing, our ordinariness. He lived as a refugee child, a schoolboy, an adolescent, a mature man, a working man, a son, a brother, a friend, a neighbour, a member of his local congregation. So ordinary in fact that his own people were hardly able to credit his public ministry because 'isn't this the carpenter's son? Isn't his mother's name Mary, and aren't his brothers James, Joseph, Simon and Judas? Aren't all his sisters with us? Where did this man get all these things?' (Matthew 13.55–6).

In Jesus, God has touched, owned and sanctified by his own presence the whole of ordinary life (indeed, can we call anything 'ordinary' since Jesus?). Here, in the incarnation of Jesus Christ, we have the answer to the neglect induced by familiarity. Bring everything which falls within your field of vision to Christ who is the expert evaluator, and discover how often a mere 'umbrella stand' is revealed to be a priceless Ming vase.

Another cause of optical distortion is *prejudice*.

We are quite unable to see those things we are biased against because we open the door of our perceptions only wide enough to allow in aspects of which we approve. Prejudice may be vicious and wilful, but more commonly it is fed and sustained by lazy ignorance. We are down on the things we are not up on. When Philip told his friend, Nathaniel, that Jesus, the Messiah, was a Nazareth man, we can feel the contempt in Nathaniel's reaction: 'Nazareth! Can anything good come from there?' He is not expecting an answer to his question. He knew Nazareth as a dull little one-horse town. His mind was made up about it: expect no surprises from Nazareth. How many times we have ourselves written off individuals, events, plans, places, in similar know-all contemptuous terms.

Philip's answer shows the way out from the warping illusions created by bias: 'Come and see!' (John 1.43–6) Expel your prejudices, your safe close-mindedness and those comfortable received opinions about people and events. Come close and look with fresh eyes and, above all else, with the humility which might allow the truth to reach you. Be willing to acknowledge that you may just be mistaking your personal myopia for normal eyesight. Come and see what God is doing here and, who knows, even unexciting and mediocre 'Nazareth' might astonish you yet.

Another reason why we fail to see what is in front of us is *caricature*, which is a particular form of prejudice. A caricature is a grotesque or ludicrous representation of a likeness. 'The monkey, the caricature of our species.' For some strange reason we find it easier, and certainly more entertaining, to look at certain people, groups, types, classes or nationalities, in caricature rather than in reality. Perhaps it is because once we exaggerate certain features to make those people appear laughable and, if at all possible, slightly ridiculous, they seem less of a challenge to us.

We travel with our social survival-kit of stock caricatures. Thus we know that 'all Yorkshire people are ...' and 'all high church clergy are ...' and 'Americans always ...'. How convenient for us this is, if we can deal with the world from the comfort of our mental armchair. It saves us the hard spiritual work of actually paying attention, looking at and listening to other people.

Most people have their store of experiences when caricature gave way to true sightedness. Let me throw in one of my own.

My wife and I were staying at a Christian Guest House in Switzerland. The manager suggested we share a table at mealtimes with 'three retired German ladies'. Tremendous, I thought, what a holiday this will be! The fact that I had never personally had any previous dealings with 'retired German ladies' was no problem for my British instinct for caricature. I had them immediately pictured in my head. They would be worthy *Hausfrauen*, humourless, efficient, very dutiful, dedicated to the German tradition of 'Küche–Kinder–Kirche', cooking, children and church. And as for their involvement in the Hitler youth and other horrors . . . We British know these things to be true of 'retired German ladies'.

In the event they were hilarious. Bright, funny, modern, attractive, adventurous and full of energy. As they tried out their elementary English language on us we were, at times, noisy enough to draw mildly disapproving glances from the other guests. We called the three 'the Golden Girls' after the glamorous stars in a popular American TV series. Our friends had come through harrowing wartime and Russian-occupation experiences as young people. They were vibrant, exploring Christians, wide awake to all kinds of faith-sharing ventures back home in Munich.

But how close I came to not 'seeing' those three lovely people because of my self-satisfied, lazy, pre-caricaturing of them. We need to unsee in order to see one another. Lord, heal my squinting soul.

CHAPTER 4

Slow looking

ᴥᴥᴥ

It is just about impossible to buy a copy of yesterday's newspaper. 'News' which only a few hours earlier was screaming for our attention in world-stopping headlines has disappeared without a trace. Here today, pulp tomorrow. It is a revealing comment on the way we attend to things.

We fight back against the absurdity of high-speed ephemeral 'news' by taking it all with a large pinch of scepticism. Throwaway information deserves no better than throw-away attention. But we do not emerge from the process unscathed. Fast, unrooted, unverifiable, disposable 'news' erodes our powers of concentration. We lose some, at least, of our willingness to attend in any depth and for any sustained time. Hence the rise of the well-known psychology of the TV commercial 'burst', and our own evolution into human beings with the attention span of a gnat.

Shallow distractedness is our problem. It will be the ruin of us unless we give ourselves a firm talking-to about our habits of attention and concentration. We have information and knowledge in vast quantities but wisdom and understanding seep away through the cracks in our powers of concentration. One astute observer of the way we are today, Austin Farrer, has suggested that the greatest impediment to spiritual life 'is that no-one ever looks at anything at all; not so as to contemplate it, to apprehend what it is to be that thing, and plumb, if he can, the deep fact of its individual existence'. He goes on to ask for a quality of attention which arises 'from the appreciation of things which we have when we love them, and fill our

21

minds and senses with them, and feel something of the silent force and great mystery of their existence'.[1]

The world would open before our eyes if we were able to bring to it that quality of respect and commitment in our observation of it. Imagine how it would refresh marriage and family life, as well as wider circles of friendships and encounters. Our perception of creation would be enriched by unexpected interest and value.

Farrer's vision is hauntingly suggestive. His verbs glow like a handful of gems: 'Look–contemplate–apprehend–plumb–appreciate–love–fill–feel'. This is not our usual way of looking and listening. He seems to invite us into a way of observing which participates in, as though by caressing and gently handling, the life around us. We cannot do better than to meditate on these thoughts and allow their message to enter our hearts, and affect our sight and hearing.

'*No-one ever looks at anything at all.*' We are accused of shallowness and lack of seriousness in our habits of looking and listening. Images flicker on the retina; decibels pound in the ear, but that is different from the attention Farrer seeks. Jesus, of course, was even more uncompromising when he said to his disciples, 'Do you have eyes but fail to see, and ears but fail to hear?' (Mark 8.18) The context of his rebuke was their failure to comprehend his works and words. Clearly they had been thoroughly dazzled by the miracle of feeding the five thousand, but with unfocused attention. They had failed to see it for the sign it was and Christ holds them responsible for their dimness.

Consider also his words about the rewards for 'careful listening'. He said, 'Consider carefully what you hear [. . .] With the measure you use, it will be measured to you – and even more. Whoever has will be given more; whoever does not have, even what he has will be taken from him' (Mark 4.24, 25). Close, expectant attention, with our minds open to the Holy Spirit, will be blessed with enlarged capacities and powers for yet more perceptive seeing and hearing. To that extent, the effectiveness of our observation is in our own hands.

Implicit in Farrer's comment that 'no-one ever looks at anything at all' is the question of the time we are prepared to give. Shallow attention glides over things, it has a low boredom threshold. Time, we feel, is not on our side, it must be out-witted, devoured, obliterated as we move from one pleasant sensation to the next as rapidly and smoothly as possible. Frankly, we feel we have not the time to give to the sort of lingering, slow-paced observation evoked by Farrer's words. But people are fighting back. We hear, for example, of the 'Slow Eating Movement' in Italy and the US and no doubt in other countries also by now. Groups of friends covenant to refuse to be rushed through daily life! The tempo of life demands too high a price of us for what we imagine we gain by slithering over the top of things rather than considering them at depth. The 'slow eaters', as you might guess, make a conscious effort to meet regularly for meals with the agreed understanding that the event could take a couple of hours, and that leisurely conversation is as important as the food.

Farrer continues his criticism, '*not so as to contemplate it*'. Nothing is sacrosanct to the non-contemplative person. You will not find the non-contemplative flocking to join the local 'slow eaters' club. The root meaning of 'contemplate' is 'to make an open space for observation', much as we would make any other sort of open space. By clearing away the rubbish and clutter from our minds; and by turning off (or, at least, turn-ing down) the infernal play-back machine located inside the head which regurgitates, unbidden, miles of chatter from earlier in the day; and by taking a grip on the unbridled rest-lessness which has become the usual state of inner life for so many of us.

Busyness we can hardly help. That is how life is for most people and it is virtually impossible to step out of it. But restlessness kills contemplation. Restlessness is an alien invasion of our inner life which sets up its own drum-beat and tempo. The effect is inner fragmentation. Restlessness is born out of the unwise desire to attempt far too much. A seventeenth-century divine, St Vincent de Paul, wrote, 'It is a trick of the devil, which he employs to deceive good souls, to incite them to do more than they are able, in order that they may no longer be able to do anything.' An insight which speaks to our desire to be true observers.

A contemplative attitude to life (to all of life, not only religious life) raises the potential of ordinariness. It expands as well as deepens and makes more vivid and interesting the things before us. One of the Church Fathers, Tertullian, said of this process: 'If I give you a rose you will not doubt God any more, but of course, the rose has to unlock a mystical insight and appreciation.' Allowing time for the 'unlocking' to take place is what we mean by contemplation. We can apply the principle to the whole of our personal world of phenomena and experience: if you . . . fall in love, enjoy a glass of wine, the company of good friends, a piece of music, a beautiful sky, or a storm, children's laughter, a funny joke, Ely Cathedral . . . – but, of course, they have to 'unlock a mystical insight and appreciation'. Conversely, what a wasteland our interior world becomes if we allow restlessness and unbelief to smother contemplation.

And if we lose contemplation then we become like the people in Jesus' parable of the wedding banquet who were all too busy to attend. Ronald Rolheiser suggests that the parable is Jesus' way of picturing non-contemplative awareness. Each person was engaged in the perfectly legitimate activities of making a living and building a life. Yet all the time there is another parallel event going on to which we are all invited. Not an event of our making or organizing but the free gift of living fellowship with God in the midst of a teeming world in which he 'unlocks a mystical insight and appreciation' of creation.

Farrer next asks for a willingness '*to apprehend what it is to be that thing, and plumb, if he can, the deep fact of its individual existence*'.

This is to look with a penetrating sympathy, with a powerful imagination which can break out of the tightly guarded circle of one's own self-interest and enter into another's life. To enter in not necessarily in order to be able to help (help may not be required, we are not speaking here of strength looking at weakness), but in order to see what life might be, and look like, from within the other one's being.

How else could Adam fulfil his task on Naming Day in Eden? God 'brought them [all the creatures] to the man to see what he would name them' (Genesis 2.19). Until that moment creation was a piled-up, chaotic, teeming mass of life. By 'naming' each species Adam released them from confusion and commissioned them for distinct and useful existence in creation. It was an incredible act of sympathetic looking and listening by which he imaginatively entered the life of each species and told them their meaning and purpose. How fascinating that this quality of observation was Adam's first expression of his own powers and status.

Christ (the Second Adam), too, looked and listened with the power of imaginative sympathy and called his followers to practise the same. He crossed over the divine–human divide in order 'to apprehend' what it is to live inside this skin of ours and 'to plumb [. . .] the deep fact of our individual existence'. For Christ it meant nothing less than to experience the power of our human sinfulness; to apprehend and plumb our fallen existence. 'Since the children have flesh and blood, he too shared in their humanity' (Hebrews 2.14). He did the unthinkable and exposed himself to satanic fascination in order 'to burst the dazzling bubble from within', says the spiritual writer Hans Urs von Balthasar.[2]

For us the challenge of Christ's imaginative and sympathetic observation of our lives, from inside as one of us, is that we can no longer view people from a safe distance, as detached, uninvolved observers. By the way Christ looks at us, he calls us to an identification with others which transcends prejudice and distaste, as in his story of the Good Samaritan (Luke 10.25–37). That good man looked twice, we are told, at the unfortunate victim of a mugging. First, he saw him from a distance and, like the priest and the Levite before him, he could have kept away. But then comes the sympathetic, imaginative looking which compelled him to go much closer to the injured man.

Countless Christians have crossed the world, immersed themselves in strange cultures, soaked their minds in difficult languages, in order to come closer to people and express Christ's love by their efforts 'to apprehend, to plumb' another's existence. No amount of surfing the Web for information about those people will ever substitute for the Christ-like movement of identification with them.

Acquire an *'appreciation of things which we have when we love them, and fill our minds and senses with them, and feel something of the silent force and great mystery of their existence'.*

There is what is sometimes called a 'masculine' mode of perception. It is characterized by assertion, command, possession, problem-solving, a muscular and conscious attempt to master and take control of the subject. On the other hand, Farrer's words are frankly more about the 'feminine' mode of seeing and hearing. More an evocation, a perception, intuitive, and open to revelation, more a lover's invitation than the (masculine) no-nonsense interrogation. It caresses textures and dwells on tastes, lingers over scents; its words are dreamy from their repose in the deep imagination. And the 'feminine' mode, by its humble willingness to be led and taught by what it observes, is the way of wisdom.

CHAPTER 5

Expect to see owls

Picture this domestic exchange outside our house in Rutland. My wife calls me in an urgent whisper: 'Look! Over there. Can you see it?' I sigh and gaze around helplessly in all directions like a demented radar receiver. I ask, 'Where? What?' She says, 'Over there. Surely you can see it now!' I reply, 'What is it? What am I looking for? What am I meant to see?' 'An owl,' she tells me. I believe her as always and try to follow the direction of her pointing finger up towards a tree. Yes, there it is, an owl, as plain as day. It really is an owl.

It helps no end to know what we are looking for and what to expect when we peer into the heaving mass of things. And where to look for it. There are owls in that wood – expect to see owls. Similarly with our looking and listening at every level. We need to have an idea of what is out there waiting for our eyes and ears to catch up. For that reason we may turn to books, or listen to lectures, and attend to people when they describe what they have encountered out there in the world. In particular there is one decision we must make which fundamentally affects our expectations of what awaits us. Eugene Warren put it in the form of a question:

> Is it chance
> Or the dance moves the world?
> Is the world blind and dumb
> Or bloom, festal?
> A vain jest, or holy feast?[1]

The choice is between the secularist and the sacramental reading of the world. This is not an academic question. It has the most profound and life-directing implications for the way we experience the impact of the world. If spirituality is something like the total reaction of the whole person to the whole of life, the outcome for us personally will depend upon our decision and choice: a secularist or a sacramental vision of the world?

One man who interpreted life by the sacramental vision, Gerard Manley Hopkins, looked about him and described what he saw as 'All things counter, original, spare, strange'; and he traced it back to God who 'Fathers-forth' creation in all its astounding, eccentric variety.[2] Frankly, I envy him his gift of noticing the ordinary textures of life in such an interesting and suggestive way. He inspires me to step outside my front door and to look. He has alerted me to what is waiting for me ('there are owls in the wood – expect to see owls'), and yes, sure enough there it is, just as he said it would be – all things *are* counter, original, spare, strange. All things, that is, are as you would expect them to be in a world which moves as in a dance, bloom, festal, a holy feast.

Notice what we are not saying. We are not saying that Hopkins' words tell us of his feelings about the real world. They do not merely picture his sensations on looking around him. Creation is in itself counter, original, spare, strange. In the present climate, when so much artistic representation in fact represents little more than how the artist feels about something, we need to stress the truth of the objective reality of the world. John Constable said that the purpose of art (visual or verbal) is 'to please by reminding, not by deceiving'. No artistic representation can trap and hold the reality of creation – that would be a deception. At best it directs our attention beyond itself to the external, real world and to the creator at its centre. The best art honours the real world by effectively 'reminding' us of it in new, imaginative, suggestive ways.

The artist, Arikha, has described his personal discovery.

Painting is like drawing water from a well. When I was an abstract painter, I thought I was the well. I was digging down into myself looking for truth and I thought the well was bottomless. But, of course, it was all wrong. After seven years I hit the rock. I felt that all the forms I was expressing were the same forms, my forms. I soon realised that there is only one thing that is not reachable, never knowable, truly infinite, and that is the real world around us.[3]

Hopkins, too, is 'reminding' us of what the world is really like if only we will look at it and listen to it. He celebrated a world which God 'fathers-forth', an understanding which unlocks and unfolds creation before our gaze, when that gaze has been alerted to what is there to be seen: there are owls in the wood – expect to see owls.

People who look at life like that (and it is for each of us, not just for poets, lovers, and artists) have made their choice and rejected the prevailing secularist myth of a world which is meaningless beyond its physical laws which keep it ticking over as it hurtles through space like a cannon-ball, an accident of chance, 'blind and dumb', a 'vain jest'. They have found that interpretation unbearably grey and claustrophobic, like living in a small, stuffy, windowless room huddled around a 25-watt bulb. They know a better way. They embrace instead the ecstatic biblical vision of a sacramental and symbolic order which is the gift of the All-Father, upheld in being by the power and wisdom of the second person of the Holy Trinity, the Logos-Christ, and moving towards the transfiguration of all things by the presence and power of the Holy Spirit.

In this vision every atom is embraced, from finches' wings to galaxies. God brings everything into existence, bestowing upon each its meaning and purpose and declaring each thing to be 'very good' (Genesis 1.31) – meaning, 'You are just what

I intend you to be; go and be yourself and so fulfil your destiny within my purposes of ecstatic love!'

This present order teems with news of a more real world: with signs, clues, metaphors, words, symbols, visions, pathways, parables, riddles which point away beyond themselves to the All-Father. Coleridge called creation 'symbolical, one mighty alphabet for infant minds'.[4]

Paul wrote: 'For all that can be known of God lies plain before their eyes; indeed God himself has disclosed it to them. Ever since the world began his invisible attributes, that is to say his everlasting power and deity, have been visible to the eye of reason, in the things he has made' (Romans 1.19–20, REB). When creation is true to itself (the self God has gifted to each) and speaks of itself by being itself, it also bears witness to the Father-Creator and speaks eloquently of him (if we will learn to lip-read creation). Hans Urs von Balthasar suggests something of the depth and the strange, haunting, otherness of our existence:

> The earthly man already lives in eternity. The true state of affairs is *not* that this fleeting, temporal existence with all its decisions is a pure here-and-now, followed by the reward or punishment of an eternal beyond as a second existence. Rather, the two are one; one is the reverse side of the other: time is concealed eternity, and eternity is revealed time. The transfigured; paradisaical world is none other than the one in which we presently live, only contemplated with different eyes [...] During the forty days in which the Risen Lord visibly walked the earth, this very earth was paradise for him, so much so that the disciples could perceive the fragrance of the blessed garden through their own earthly dullness and they could even make us smell the fragrance through the Resurrection narratives.[5]

Those thoughts raise in our minds questions about owls in the wood waiting for our eyes to focus, our dull hearing to be attuned. What, then, can we expect to see in such a creation? What is an appropriate way to look into it?

George Herbert expressed the two understandings, the secularist and the sacramental, in his lovely metaphor of glass:

> A man who looks on glass
> On it may stay his eye
> Or, if he pleaseth, through it pass
> And then the heaven espy.[6]

The failure of the secularist vision is that it stops too soon – it loses its nerve and cannot go on to reach through to what is 'there' at the centre of all reality.

Looking at attractive glass (as in stained-glass windows in church) is an interesting enough exercise, but it misses the point. What makes the designs in the glass seeable? The light streaming in from outside. However intriguing the surface texture, and picturing, and shape of the glass, its designed purpose is to connect the observer in the pew with the sky outside. At the same instant it mediates the light from the sky to the observer. In that way glass can facilitate profound transactions which may be transforming for the worshipper 'if he pleaseth'.

What is true of glass applies to all creation. The sacramental and symbolic vision first looks at (and values and enjoys) what it sees, but then is drawn through to the glowing centre-point at the heart of all created things, the epiphany of God.

Jesus himself constantly took up the physical world around him as windows through which 'to pass' to the greater reality of the eternal world: birds, fish, seeds, plants, foxes, trees, jewellery, children, wayward sons, banquets, and so on. What does that fact suggest about the mysterious value and properties of ordinary, humdrum creation, the symbolic and sacramental potential of the familiar sights and sounds lying around us each day? And is not Austin Farrer right to call upon us to look and listen so as to 'contemplate [...] to apprehend [...] to plumb [...] to appreciate [...] to love [...] To fill our minds and senses with them [...] and feel them'? A world loaded with such potential, latent with such possibilities, is worthy of our awe and humility as we look and listen and imagine seraphim (who see and understand these things so much better than we do!) calling to each other 'Holy, holy, holy is the Lord Almighty; the whole earth is full of his glory' (Isaiah 6.3).

There are owls in the wood – expect to see owls. The glory of God fills the whole earth – expect to see the glory of God.

But what does the 'glory of God' look like? Would we recognize it if we saw it? By way of a response to those questions we visit a dance.

When those great theological thinkers, the Greek Fathers, meditated on the relationship between God the Father, the Son and the Holy Spirit, they saw it as an ecstatic dance of self-surrendering love, and coined the word *perichoresis*, a dance which moves in a circle (*choreo* is the Greek word for 'dance' from which we get our 'choreography'). By this image they tried to suggest the mutual delight and love between the persons of the Trinity, a giving and receiving, a movement towards and from, as in a dance. In this profound doctrine they imagined Father, Son and Holy Spirit eternally serving each other in a mutual, reciprocal bestowing, an exchange as in a dance, in which every movement of one partner is answered and balanced by the harmonious response of the other.

In the dynamic symbol of the *perichoresis*, the divine power is expressed not as sheer, irresistible, coercive force, but rather as the power and the will to give oneself totally in inexhaustible and self-surrendering love for the delight of the other. Ecstatic love (a going out of oneself in love) pours out for the other in which all is giving and there is no thought of taking; what one has is the gift of the other.

The divine dance of ecstatic love cannot, by its nature, be

contained. It overflows into creation. Why the world? Not because God the Holy Trinity *needs* it. Father, Son and Spirit are wholly self-sufficient, from eternity to all eternity, within their mutual love and delight. But such love is irrepressible, outpouring, overflowing; the dance will not be contained but bursts out into cosmic creation, into God's 'let there be . . .' and his 'let us make human beings in our image' (Genesis 1.3, 26, REB). Why the world? Because God is ecstatic, boundless love. What, then, is the fundamental stuff of creation, its driving power, and its purpose and destiny? Love.

In love the Holy Trinity opened up the Dance to make space, infinite space, for the cosmos to enter and join the dance ('In my Father's house are many rooms' – John 14.2). How, then, should we look at this world and what should we expect to see and hear? What owls are there in these woods? What respect, attention, praise, hope, are appropriate for such a spectacle in a creation irradiated by the ecstatic love of the Trinity? We should surely look at the world in its transparency to its fiery heart and the beckoning God of love.

CHAPTER 6

Before Talk

ℒ ℒ ℒ

At this point you are wondering whatever became of the tongue. It is all very well our celebrating the gifts of sight and hearing as activities near to the heart of what it means to be human, but speech has no less that same mystical quality. Indeed it has. The Genesis writer recognizes man's privilege as lying simply in the fact that of all creatures he is allowed to speak (Genesis 2.18–23).

But the 'wisdom'-teachers in scripture are clear that speech must not be allowed to thrust itself into precedence. 'He who answers before listening – that is his folly and his shame' (Proverbs 18.13) is a typical judgement. Israel's entire approach to attaining wisdom was built on the primacy of the ear over the tongue.

Words are powerful and unstable things. Once out of our mouths they are off into circulation, beyond recall, with potential for good or evil. Or they lie around like unexploded bombs embedded in life (James 3.1–12). Make sure, therefore, the wisdom-teachers advise, that you do not become just one more word-mill, moved by any passing breeze into churning out words upon words upon words in a tedious over-production which merely devalues all your words.

From scripture's wisdom tradition we are given two star personalities who enact profound listening and revelatory seeing – Solomon and Job. We cannot do better than ponder their experience.

What would you ask for if allowed to ask for anything? When God invited Solomon (1 Kings 3.5–12) to name 'whatever you want me to give you' we have a glimpse of the man's renowned wisdom. Not longevity, wealth, fame, success over his enemies – he reached instead behind those secondary blessings for the gift which is seminal to wise and fruitful action. He asked for the gift of a 'discerning heart' (vv. 9, 12), which is literally a 'listening' or 'hearing' heart. In Hebrew understanding the heart is the place for thinking, perception, reasoning, reflecting, considering. It is as much intellectual activity as emotional. In fact our usual metaphorical use of 'heart' as the place of moods and deepest feelings is not the biblical one at all.

What exactly did Solomon's 'listening' heart listen for? He did not covet our modern, authoritative, hard-edged reason which dominates natural life, but asked instead for an 'understanding' reason which resonates with, and is in sympathy with, the phenomena he observes. The 'hearing' heart has an attuned sensitivity for the truth which emanates from the world and calls to humankind.

It is important to realize that Solomon was not asking for 'spiritual' gifts of listening in an exclusively 'spiritual' sense. That idea of a split between the physical and the spiritual is unknown in scripture. God is one and his creation is one. God will come to us in whatever way and through whatever media he chooses, including natural phenomena and the events which occur on that particular stage. 'Creation is a hand reaching straight into experience and arranging it with new meaning.'[1] As Professor Jacob Bronowski put it, it is one of God's hands (how else can he touch us?), one of his many dialects. And it was this whole created order that Solomon wanted to hear speaking.

A wise man's heart guides his mouth, (Proverbs 16.23), and he is wise because he listens. Fullness of perception arises out of receptive hearing. Solomon coveted an expanding capacity for hearing, which makes for a wise and discerning heart. Attentive hearing increases the 'breadth' of the heart and mind. In Solomon's case it enabled him to grasp the fullness of natural and social phenomena. At this point we can best switch from 'heart' to 'mind': Solomon observed with a penetrating, organizing intelligence such things as international culture, scholarship and scientific inquiries (into botany, zoology, education theory, politics, law). He was famed for his powers of accurate judgement and for his poetic language (1 Kings 4.29–34). He 'listened' for the distinctions between good and evil in practical government (1 Kings 3.9).

But we would be seriously mistaken if we imagined the 'listening, hearing heart' to be a state of inert, passive receptivity, as if such a mind is a screen on to which understanding is projected. The activities of 'listening, hearing, discerning' in wisdom teaching refer to highly focused, intense engagements with the oncoming truth. Our Bible reading, therefore, far from being a dreamy, serene affair, should rather leave us feeling as though we had just dug over a fair-size vegetable garden.

Next we turn to Job whose experience could not have been more different from Solomon's. In flat contradiction of everything we have said about the priority of observation over speaking, Job chattered endlessly, pouring a dense verbal fog over his situation: chapter upon chapter upon chapter, mostly in complaint against God's management of Job's life.

When at last God answers Job's accusations against his goodness and justice he does so in an astonishing manner fascinating to anyone interested in the divine range and repertoire of communication. He leads Job outside and says, 'Look!' Rest your tongue, use your eyes. Creation parades past in a stunning carnival. Here is Job's answer if only he will look and interpret the spectacle. Clearly God has complete confidence in his creatures that in speaking of themselves they will speak faithfully of God to Job.

Everything is on show (38.1—42.65): snowflakes, galaxies, wild donkeys, the wonderful and the weird, the funny and the frightful, the delicate and the dangerous, the fragile and the ferocious. The only words spoken are God's stream of counter-questions fired off in machine-gun bursts designed to focus Job's attention on the reality passing before him: Were you there? Do you know? Can you tell? Have you ever? Teach me – God is saying to Job – you who are so clever and have lived so long, seen everything, and understand so much about the way the world proceeds. A slight frisson of uncertainty creeps into Job's attitudes.

But God's trust that creation can argue his case for him is truly remarkable. It invites us (with Job) to look into the world and understand. *First*, by reading the signs and clues, the symbolism of created things which mirrors their maker; and *second*, by honesty in the face of impenetrable mystery. Creation can lead the humble, seeking observer so far, but from then on progress will be made only by faith in God's revealing word.

We are learning here that in our own place and time we, as much as Job, need to scan creation with the same double objective: to understand what the created order is empowered to say to us, and to acknowledge the mystery which is beyond our reach.

What went on in Job's mind as he stood there with the world marching past for his inspection? The variety is incredible. So much difference running free within a controlling order. The way creation is witnesses to design and purpose, intention and orderliness which allow life to thrive. It speaks of foundations laid carefully before superstructures (38.4–6), of boundaries, limits and discipline (8–11), of a framework which allows nature to run freely and joyously in fruitfulness and harvest: in a word, government.

Obviously, chapters 38—42 are a poet's description. Everything in God's speech is poetic; nothing in it is technical, philosophical or specialist at all. Everyman's language is used to communicate with Everyman. Job is invited to look at the dawn when the earth 'takes shape like clay under a seal' (38.14) and to ponder the significance (the 'sign') of its sheer

unfailing regularity by which God sustains all life. A faithful
creation testifies to its faithful creator (Genesis 8.22), who is
covenant-keeping, wise and life-giving. Why then should we
imagine that such a God will ever be less in his relationships
with us? Look, interpret, believe – then go in hope and joy.

Job is watching the procession go past him, delighted with
every evidence of humour and surprise. Why did God ever
bother to create in the first place, and now tirelessly sustain
his handiwork in overflowing, bountiful life? For the joy
and the love of it (see above on the Dance of the Trinity, the
perichoresis, in chapter 5). Christ as pre-existent 'wisdom'
(Proverbs 8.22–31) is pictured as a high-spirited child who
delights to sport with the human family in the playground of
the world. Expect to see evidence of that wondrous child in
the way the world is. The ostrich, for example, (39.13–18) who
has the last laugh however stupid and ugly she is, because of
her lightning acceleration and her kick like a cannon. And
what are we to make of those two who so intrigued God that
half of chapter 40 and the whole of 41 are given over to their
delicious descriptions: the hippopotamus and the crocodile?

Look at how youngsters react at the zoo when they set
eyes on those two strange creatures. They are fascinated and
frightened, awestruck and amused. Can you seriously look a
hippo or a croc in the eye and solemnly claim to understand
the imagination of their designer? God's commentary whispers
in Job's ear that a man can no more tame the intentions of God
than a small child can lead a crocodile on a piece of string (41.5).

And creation can play the fool. Perhaps by now the animal
jokers in the carnival were thoroughly 'out of hand' with their
antics. Much that goes on out there seems to be just for the
extravagant fun of it, put on presumably for our delight and
worthy of our protection and respect. The world is full of
odd-ball characters both in the animal realm and in our own!
Laughter is itself a 'creature', a small one, which enjoys special
status in heaven. The Psalmist saw laughter as the reflection

and likeness of God's feelings about affairs on earth (Psalm 2). A good laugh is a sign of God. Real, side-splitting laughter originates in heaven. Our jokes, when good jokes, point the way back to the place of the very best, the funniest humour. Jürgen Moltmann reminds us that 'the glorification of God lies in the demonstrative joy of existence'.[2] So much in the created order dances about us, inviting us to join in the laughter.

The great war-horse galloped past Job (39.19–25), provoking thoughts of the power and majesty of God. Laugh at the monkey, play with the snow, throw stones at the mountain goat if you must, but it would be most unwise to upset the great horse: huge, beautiful, brave, fleet, powerful. The description is so tense and excited, so overwhelmed in admiration of the creature's magnificence, that our imaginations which thrive on the symbolical, are delighted to take it for the creator's grace and strength. Add to that the 'laws of the heavens' which are within 'God's dominion' (38.33). They witness to an energy and an expansive, designing mind beyond our comprehension. Will such a God act in a feckless, arbitrary manner with his people?

The poem turns to signs of God's irrepressible freedom in the symbol of the hawk and the eagle as they soar and glide (39.26–30). Meanwhile, the earth-bound wild donkey and wild ox (39.5–12), renowned for their untameable stubbornness, mock our efforts to break them in for domestic use. The crocodile also is symbolic of unharnessed ferocity: 'If you lay a hand on him, you will remember the struggle and never do it again!' (41.8) Look at the world, then, and read the clues concerning your relationship with God. The message of the carnival is plain: God cannot be snared by our arguments or caught by our theories and schemes. We will never be able to trap and domesticate the Almighty. Creation is dancing around us, a multi-media demonstration of divine freedom. Take it to heart, and give up your rash, ignorant judgements on the judge of all creation.

If Job is still on his feet, there are other lessons being enacted before him in the parade. One of Job's criticisms of God's ways with him is that he, Job, seems to be of no value or significance in the divine scheme of things. 'He throws me into the mud, and I am reduced to dust and ashes' is a typical moan (30.19). In the poem God answers by pointing Job to the individual distinctiveness of every creature in the procession. Each one is differently 'counter, original, spare, strange'. And each one after its own manner adds something unique and valuable to creation's ecstatic celebration of God. In one of his sermons Gerard Manley Hopkins said: 'The birds sing to him, the thunder speaks of his terror, the lion is like his strength, the sea is like his greatness, the honey like his sweetness; they are something like him, they make him known, they tell of him, they give him glory.'

The thrust of God's great poem is 'Look! . . . Look! . . . Look! Let creation minister wisdom to you.'

Even before he had reached this climax of revelation, Job had earlier intuited the same principle in thoughts very similar to those of Hopkins:

> But ask the beasts, and they will teach you;
> ask the birds of the air to inform you,
> or tell the creatures that crawl to teach you,
> and the fish of the sea to instruct you.
> Who does not come to know from all these
> that the hand of the Lord has done this?
>   (Job 12.7–9, REB)

We are back with remarks made at the end of the first chapter, that humility is wisdom's inseparable twin and essential for penetrating, perceptive seeing. If on the other hand we look upon the world with the attitude of arrogant domination sadly typical of our pragmatic secularism, we shall never hear, or see, its witness to God. The humble, teachable spirit will discern what God has hidden of himself in creation.

But the carnival has even more to say to Job. It does not portray a cuddly Disneyland idea of the world but an utterly real one. It is a tough place in which life can be a rough experience. The eagle's 'young ones feast on blood' (39.30). That's the way it is. And there is also the mysterious presence of malign spiritual forces which must be acknowledged and dealt with if our view of the world is not to be hopelessly romantic and naïve. Therefore, central to the poem's world-view are those two icons of disorder, chaos and threat, 'Behemoth' and 'Leviathan', masquerading as the hippopotamus (40.15) and the crocodile (41.11) splashing around in the swamps.

In Babylonian mythology Behemoth and Leviathan were the primeval monsters of chaos, Tiamat and Kingu. In the Hebrew apocalyptic tradition, Behemoth and Leviathan were 'cast the one into the abyss of the sea, and the other into the dryland of the wilderness [. . .] these two monsters [. . .] will be food for all the righteous who remain'.[3] Scripture agrees: 'In that day, the Lord [. . .] will slay the monster of the sea' ('Leviathan' – Isaiah 27.1).

Meanwhile the penny had dropped with a great clang inside Job's head. He saw . . . well, *something* which convinced him that God could be trusted with the outcome of his life: a humbling realization that he had glimpsed just a fraction of the mysterious, incomprehensible, but utterly trustworthy majesty of God. What he could see and understand, however little, convinced him that he could believe God for the rest. Creation takes us only so far and then slips away out of our grasp, elusive, teasing, suggestive, a taste of greater things to come:

> These [God's mighty deeds] are but the outer fringe of
>   his works;
>   How faint the whisper we hear of him!
>   Who then can understand the thunder of his power?
>   (Job 26.14)

The carnival was able to tell Job only so much. It did not solve the problem of undeserved suffering but made the problem more luminous. The 'answer' awaits the advent of Jesus Christ: 'When a composer such as God creates the opera of the world and places in its centre his crucified and risen Son, every fault-finding at his work, i.e. whether or not he could have done it better, must be reduced to silence.'[4]

But Job had seen enough. Careful looking (at what is always there in the world, passing before our unfocused eyes) did what his much speaking never could. He emerged reeling from the encounter with God in his creation, born again:

Then Job replied to the Lord:

'I know that you can do all things;
no plan of yours can be thwarted.
You asked, "Who is this that obscures my counsel without
knowledge?"
Surely I spoke of things I did not understand,
things too wonderful for me to know

You said, "Listen now, and I will speak;
I will question you,
and you shall answer me."
My ears had heard of you
but now my eyes have seen you.
Therefore I despise myself
and repent in dust and ashes.'

(Job 42.1–6)

CHAPTER 7

'Here and now, boys'

The mynah birds in Aldous Huxley's story 'Island' are trained to flutter down on unsuspecting humans with the cry 'Attention! Here and now, boys, here and now.' The young islander, Mary Sarojini MacPhail, explains to a startled newcomer who had just received the mynah treatment that the birds do so because 'That's what you always forget, isn't it? I mean, you forget to pay attention to what's happening.' Smart girl. She opens yet another window on a principle which has appeared in each of our meditations so far: the importance of observing the present moment.

Wisdom, according to Miss MacPhail, is the whole person wholly attending to what is contained at this time on this particular bit of the earth's surface.

Christians in eighteenth-century France rated the spiritual potential of the here and now so highly that they spoke of it as 'the sacrament of the present moment'. Just as the Lord comes to his people under cover of bread and wine in holy communion, and in water at baptism, so also the will of God comes to us within this present here-and-now moment. What is the will of God for you? That question is answered by another one: What do you see in this present moment? What awaits your attention? What opportunities for love, service, action are there in it?

When Jesus promised his people, 'I will never leave you or forsake you', he claimed mastery over each here-and-now circumstance. It means that life arrives second by second having passed through the Lord's hands and freighted with his love and purposes. It means also that with each situation something is laid before you which calls for faith and decision. There is a will of God for every event we encounter. Various responses are possible for you. You may choose to avoid taking action. We blame others, we complain that the situation is too complicated or too big, we turn our backs, close our eyes, even tell lies. But in the end we are free to do only one of two things, either to step into this moment and welcome it as containing the will of God, or to back away from it. Either way, we make our decision. 'Attention! Here and now, boys, here and now' means entering the present moment with eyes wide open.

The first thing to be said about the present moment is that God has *called* us into it. It is never our own powers or abilities which redeem the here and now, but the fundamental fact that God has *called* us to the life he has set us to live. Christians complain that they feel ineffectual, out-numbered, out-gunned, marginalized in society. The answer lies not in yet more activism but in first recovering our sense of call to participate in God's purpose (Ephesians 4.1). The uncanny teaching of the New Testament is that God 'chose' us in Christ 'before the creation of the world' (Ephesians 1.4), and having in the mystery of his grace and wisdom chose us he put his choice into action by 'calling' us to himself by the word and touch of the Holy Spirit in our hearts (Romans 8.29, 30). For some people the realization of God's call was like an inner explosion. For others, and it seems this is more usual, the call has appeared as a quiet dawning whisper. The level of excitement is incidental. What matters is that God's effective call in our hearts has transformed everything, especially the way we look at and listen to the here and now.

God's will is already out there, ahead of us each day waiting for us to catch up with it. Paul describes it as 'good works which God prepared in advance for us to do' (Ephesians 2.10). We encounter those 'good works' throughout the day as they unfold in the flow of successive 'present moments'. It means that with his call God has given us his Midas touch. The boring, the routine, the drab and humdrum turn to gold when received from God and used for him.

Notice what this wonderful truth does to the way we look at our Monday to Friday working life. First, if every Christian is 'called' then every Christian has a vocation, a calling. You have a vocation which is to live the life God has set you to live. Within that sphere you meet the will of God. For about a thousand years the Church lost sight of this truth and we are still infected by wrong ideas of vocation. The 'monastic' domination of calling persists tenaciously in various forms and shades. There was a time when only certain 'special' groups and practitioners of high-prestige occupations were regarded as having a vocation: theology, medicine, law, monastic life, missionary life. The rest of the population simply had 'jobs', trades, and led 'ordinary lives'. Thus a disastrous split occurred in the minds of Christian people. A few had a vocation, they were 'called', while the great majority were relegated to spiritually second-class citizens. You can see how such an understanding subverted, for most people, the emancipating joy of living by 'the sacrament of the present moment'.

In that hurtful dualism the 'sacred' was valued above the 'secular'; the ordained above the lay; the celibate above the married; Latin above the common tongue; the extraordinary above the ordinary; activities in Church above those outside. And what was termed the 'perfect' (monastic) life rated as spiritually superior to the 'permitted' life of the vast majority of people.

One side-effect of that dualistic view, which still plagues us today, is a limited and special idea of evangelism as properly left to those 'called' to ministry. Yet the New Testament reveals a wonderfully more free and dynamic picture in which everyone is in everything everywhere, as salt and light. Each Christian is called to a wholly integrated life revolving around the one centre which is to glorify and enjoy God in *all things*. Thus the great cry of the scriptures about the priesthood of all believers: 'You [i.e. all Christian] are a chosen people, a royal priesthood, a holy nation, a people belonging to God' (1 Peter 2.9). The corollary of that tremendous statement is that if *all* are priests then the work of all is priestly work. *All* work. Your usual work is your calling and your spiritual work, for it is the sphere in which you live to please God. Tyndale said, 'Between the washing of dishes and the preaching of the word there is a difference. But concerning pleasing God there is no difference at all.'

Martin Luther said, 'We are priests in our own tasks, in our everyday work.' No doubt he had in mind Paul's words, 'Whatever you do, work at it with all your heart, as working for the Lord, not for men' (Colossians 3.23). And here is Luther again, urging us to look at the work under our hand as a priest looks at his altar: 'Look around your workshop, at your hammer and nails. These are messengers from God. Use them as a means of serving and loving your God and your neighbour.' Priestly work is pleasing God and loving our neighbour, whatever the particular task may be.

Where is the will of God within the sacrament of the here and now? Among your 'tools' and in your daily work of hand and brain. This calls for deliberate preparation each morning as we face the new day. Reach out your empty hands and by faith receive the coming day as God's new gift, precious, unique, brimming with potential because it contains such scope for doing his will. How foolish it would be to launch into the day's work and opportunities day-dreaming about being someone else somewhere else. We need the urgent reminder, 'Attention! Here and now, boys, here and now.'

But we do feel a stubborn tension between doing our so-called 'ordinary' work and what we are pleased to refer to as 'Christian' or 'spiritual' work. Vestiges of the old sacred/secular dualism persist, even in the evangelical and charismatic heart-land. An interesting example of its latest manifestation is in the generally helpful materials on the use of spiritual gifts produced by the Church Growth Movement in the US. Christians are encouraged to acknowledge the gifts of the Holy Spirit which they have and to seek other gifts. The dual-ism appears when we ask where these gifts are to be used: answer, within the life of the local churches, as if the Holy Spirit has less concern for the immense spiritual needs in wider society outside the church. Thus a new elite emerges within the churches. Church life breaks even further away from its local world. False ideas of what 'real living' is about flourish. The will of God becomes more and more a church-centred concern. It is yet another example of the old, deep, divide between sacred and secular which Christ, in a human body, came to heal.

If we will heed Huxley's mynah birds and attend to our daily life as it comes to us moment by moment and in forms which contain the will of God, we will be on the way towards genuine contentment of heart. Our usually fragmented, and therefore frustrating, existence can be gathered around the acceptance of who we are at this moment, where we are and what our work is. This way leads to the recovery of personal meaning within a vision of life, our life, as having priestly (God-pleasing) significance. The doctrine of the Christ-of-the-present-moment reintegrates our interior world.

To summarize: What do we see as we look at our personal daily world? We see that 'the daily round and common task' by which we earn our bread and butter is the sphere of our calling. We see also that the inevitable boredom and drabness in much of the routine is redeemed when seen as (and this is the transforming miracle) a vehicle for the will of God. We see then that we are 'priests in our own tasks, in our everyday work [. . .] Look around your workshop'.

Let us be clear about what we are *not* claiming for this spirituality of the here and now. It does not require us to give full concentration to every face we see throughout the day, or to scrutinize for hidden meanings every empty crisp packet blowing down the street! Far from that sort of strained, rather manic obsessiveness, what is required of us is an awareness, an alertness, a sensitivity to the potential of the here and now. The Lord does not work in a uniform way, at the same pace or fixed voltage. He is not simply 'there', unchanging, like the pattern on the wallpaper or like gravity. Within the vision of ourselves and our days as 'priests' in our own tasks, in our everyday work, there are moments and occasions when in the rhythm of the Holy Spirit things come together and peak. Moments of possibility set up by the Holy Spirit. Moments which await our perceptive seeing and hearing.

Jesus spoke of this intuitive observation of our local, daily world by the metaphor of sky-scanning and weather forecasting. 'When you see a cloud rising in the west, immediately you say, "It's going to rain," and it does. And when the south wind blows, you say, "It's going to be hot," and it is. Hypocrites! You know how to interpret the appearance of the earth and the sky. How is it that you don't know how to interpret this present time?' (Luke 12.54–6) Looking and listening, supported by all the senses, those 'talismans of the Lord' are regarded by Jesus as activities of spiritual intelligence-gathering. 'You see [. . .] you interpret the appearance [. . .] interpret the present time'.

The word translated 'present time' is *kairos*, which means timing, timeliness, as when a saucepan of milk comes to the boil; or fruit, just ripe for picking; or shares just right for selling. The Christ-of-the-present-moment is the Christ of perfect timing as he moves in our affairs. In practical terms what does this mean for our daily life? First, I go into the day having accepted as a gift both my own existence and the day ahead with its 'good works', which God prepared in advance for us to do (Ephesians 2.10). There is a will of God for each hour, each phase and each occurrence throughout the day. I go, therefore, praying in my heart for discernment. Within a prayerful heart and mind certain impressions arise: I feel I should pray for that colleague over there; I have a sense that I ought to call on a neighbour to ask about her sick mother; I find myself in conversation with another acquaintance at work over lunch and our talk turns to a programme on TV the evening before in which a survivor from a rail crash described how she prayed while trapped in the wreckage. So the day unfolds: no strain, no artificial engineering of encounters with people, no forced, mutually embarrassing 'witnessing'. Rather a sense of prayerfully walking behind the Lord through the day responding to his *kairos* in situations he invites us into. Let me add a personal experience which made a great impression on me at the time as an instance of having one's gaze 'directed', as I believed, by the Holy Spirit.

It was in a border town between Malaysia and Thailand. A boom town in which accommodation suitable for a family was just about impossible to obtain. In fact we were renting part of a failed night club-brothel, a dismal place, unhealthy for the family and unsuitable for our work of evangelism in a Buddhist-Muslim society. We were praying continuously for a better place. One day I was cycling towards the river through a pleasant Malay part of the town when quite suddenly I felt I had to stop. A detector somewhere inside my head had 'seen' something. Certainly I was not at the time consciously looking for clues to new accommodation. I went back up the road to see what it was that had seized (subconsciously) my attention. It was a smudge of white in the grass on the edge of the road outside a Malay house. I went closer to look: fresh wood shavings. Someone was working inside the house and the only clue was these few shavings.

I went in and found a Malay builder renovating this attractive, simple house which had a pleasant garden at the back. One thing led to another and a few hours later our prayers were answered: we were renting a house we came to love and which was perfect for our work. It was a classic '*kairos*' moment: our need and God's provision coming together; my cycle ride past the house when the wood shavings were there and before the rain washed them away into the monsoon drain at the front of the house; a friendly landlord: 'You see . . . You interpret the appearance . . . interpret the present time.' Within the whole teeming humming mass of things which make up daily life there are 'fresh wood shavings' trying to catch our eye. This is such a vital part of our looking and listening that it deserves exploring a little further in the next chapter.

CHAPTER 8

'Our eyes by seeing learn to see'

There is a word for that 'fresh wood shavings' incident described at the end of the previous chapter. A word for the uncanny experience of certain impressions attracting our attention as they seem to call or wave to us from out of a crowd of things. The word is 'wisdom'.

Already wisdom has figured as a key player in our explorations of what goes on when we look or listen (in chapters 1 and 6). In scripture Wisdom is not a philosophical category but a person (Proverbs 8.22–31). It is like a playful laughing child 'rejoicing in his [God's] whole world and delighting in mankind' (v. 31), and is pictured also as a woman who

> [...] [C]alls aloud in the street,
>   she raises her voice in the public squares;
> at the head of the noisy streets she cries out,
>   in the gateways of the city she makes her speech [...]
>   (Proverbs 1.20–1)

If you have ever stood in a busy Near Eastern market you will appreciate how 'Wisdom' would have to strive to make herself heard! But she is heard by the humble-minded and attentive. They detect her voice, and catch her signal, coming out from the competing, jostling mayhem of the market place.

There is a beautiful celebration of Wisdom in the apocryphal book of Sirach (or Ecclesiasticus):

> She [Wisdom] will come out to meet him [the attentive seeker] like a mother;
> she will receive him like a young bride. (15.2)

Another is in the Wisdom of Solomon: 'She [Wisdom] is easily discerned by those who love her, and by those who seek her she is found [. . .] For she herself ranges in search of those who are worthy of her; on their daily path she appears to them with kindly intent, and in all their purposes she comes toward them in every thought' (6.12, 16).

The New Testament brings wisdom teaching to full bloom. The Wisdom celebrated in Proverbs, Psalms, Job etc. is identified as the second person of the Holy Trinity, our Lord Jesus Christ 'in whom are hidden all the treasures of wisdom and knowledge' (Colossians 2.3). He it is who 'calls out' from among the buzzing swarm of things, and promises to 'come out' to the attentive seeker, so that we find ourselves drawn to particular things or people.

What I experienced as I cycled down that Thai village street was a whisper in the head saying, 'Hold on. Something odd back there. What was it? A sprinkling of white, fresh, new. Go back and look again.' The scriptures we have quoted show Wisdom always ahead of us, scanning the road, calling, signalling, directing those who stay alert to Wisdom's counsel. 'Wisdom is proved right by all her children' (Luke 7.35).

Just how we are drawn to look or listen to one thing among so much else is part of Wisdom's mysterious arts. We find it very difficult to describe precisely, because it is not the least bit precise. We use terms like feeling, gut-feeling, a touch, a hunch, or even an itch! In the end all we can say is 'I just felt I had to . . .' If I may speak personally, I have come to trust a sensation which is something like a slight twinge of indigestion. This I have learned is how I first intuit wisdom's signal that I need to change a course of action.

Or perhaps it is like a needle coming within a magnetic field; there occurs a tremor, a slight movement, a clue to an invisible presence. Syntonization may be another way of picturing the way we come under wisdom's direction. Syntonization occurs when a note sounded on one instrument produces the corresponding note on another instrument; or like a child drawn into a little dance as she listens to music. Or when a stick is thrown into a turbulent stream and takes on the movement of the water. Syntonization happens when a greater energy is repeated, in its own distinctive way, in a lesser energy. The energy of love, which is also God's wisdom, is reproduced in us, the instruments of lesser energy, as impressions, a stress, a touch, a push, or simply as an indefinable sense that 'I ought to . . .'.

Lovers will swear that it is possible to be in a crowd of people and feel, become strangely aware of, someone there. Their presence draws one person's attention their way. But presumably the two people involved in that mysterious psychic exchange are somehow emotionally synchronized. Even so, it suggests to the rest of us that our own state of heart and mind does matter in relation to wisdom's communications. We, as much as any lovers, will go through the day spiritually synchronized with the Wisdom who 'calls aloud in the street'. So that as countless images and words stream towards us out of our local world we are able to intuit Christ's touch, his wave, his whisper in certain of them.

If I may be allowed to give another personal example (they are always the best ones! That is, the writer can quote them with full sincerity and conviction, which is no bad thing): A congregation of which I was minister at the time had the pleasant task of adjusting to growth. The question seemed to come down to bricks and mortar and the need to extend the premises. I was feeling one of my 'mild twinges of indigestion' about this prospect yet had no clear idea of a better plan. At the end of one Sunday morning service, I made my way through the usual crush of people having coffee and repossessing their children in the hall. As I was squeezing past a group of people chatting together I overheard a scrap of a sentence, '. . . then we must send people elsewhere'. It hit me like a revelation. Of course! Don't extend the buildings but start another congregation elsewhere (this was before the 'church planting' movement in the UK was so fashionable). I am convinced that the Lord-who-is-our-wisdom called through those few words spoken in the midst of thousands of other words 'at the head of the noisy streets [...] in the gateways of the city', in a crowded church hall after the morning service.

Our looking and listening are rooted in the life of the indwelling Holy Spirit of revelation. 'Things beyond our seeing, things beyond our hearing, things beyond our imagining' the Spirit reveals to his alert, aware, synchronized people (1 Corinthians 2.9, REB). The Holy Spirit is the Lord of light; he deals in illumination and disclosure; he reveals the mind of the Father; he is Christ's Holy Spirit of Wisdom who draws our seeing and hearing his way.

In other words our observation requires intuition linked to reflective thought. You feel your attention seized by something. It reaches out for you and grasps you as you pass. It calls out from the seething throng of impressions. Coleridge, who was an awesomely profound observer, said of the process, 'I no sooner felt than I sought to understand.' First feel the impression, then try to understand what you have felt. Perhaps the best demonstration of the principle is found in the strange case of Moses at the burning bush.

It would be difficult to imagine a less promising situation for Moses. His brilliant career prospects wrecked back in Egypt, here he is looking after sheep on 'the far side of the desert' (Exodus 3.1). Another hot, tedious, humdrum day in the desolate outback of the ancient Near East. This is life in its most basic ordinariness, apparently utterly unspiritual, no promise anywhere of divine intervention. Just sand, scrub and silly, bleating sheep.

Then he notices a bush on fire. Nothing very remarkable about that in such a climate and those conditions. At this

point the future existence of Israel (and her mission) as the
covenant people of God, and that of the Exodus, are in the
balance. How long will Moses stand there watching the fire?
Will he stay, or leave and catch up with his sheep? Producers
of TV commercials calculate our interest span to be about a
couple of minutes maximum before we reach for the programme selector and search for something more entertaining.
In which case we would have failed the test God set Moses.

How long would Moses need to stand watching the fire
before it dawned on him that something strange was going
on there? It depends upon the size of the bush! Say, some
fifteen minutes. When did you last look intently at something
as ordinary as a fire for fifteen minutes, without falling
asleep?

We can only guess at Moses' thoughts as he watched:
interest, curiosity, attention, a growing unease and incredulity,
excitement and fear, an impression of witnessing something
uncanny and eerie, a coming under the sway of the spectacle,
of being drawn in until 'I will go over and see this strange
sight – why the bush does not burn up' (Exodus 3.3). So far
God has not uttered a word but allows Moses' sight to lead
him. As Dante wrote, 'My eyes by seeing learned to see.'

Clearly God was exploring Moses' qualities. Was the man
curious and interested in the phenomena around him? Was he
imaginative, did he have an experimental attitude to life, was
he inquisitive, expectant, hopeful, focused enough to pay
attention to an emerging signal for a few minutes without
collapsing back into lethargy? These, apparently, are the qualities which can discern the Lord within events.

And then there is the fire itself. Looking into a fire is not a
bit like looking at a computer screen. The machine produces
crisp, unambiguous, manageable images. Fire, on the other
hand, is a blaze forever changing its appearances, a sponta-
neous dazzle, a blur, a shining confusion, a symbol of the
divine presence, and a clue to the inventiveness of God's

approaches – always at work within our affairs but never once repeating himself. But we should not over-rate the fire. The fire is not God nor is it the glory of God, but in a symbolic and sacramental creation fire (like all phenomena) is transparent to God, created with the potential to serve its creator as a medium for his actions. The writer of the apocryphal Book of Esdras expressed it in striking words: 'Your glory passed through the four gates of fire and earthquake and wind and ice, to give the law to the descendants of Jacob' (2 Esdras 3.19). The Lord chose to approach Moses through fire as a gate; then and only then, he spoke.

The burning bush encounter demonstrates God's sovereign freedom to choose when and how he comes to us. Never limit him by saying 'God couldn't possibly speak to me out of this situation', nor try to coerce him by insisting that 'of course, the Lord always works like this and this'. Hands off! Let God be God. His repertoire of approaches is unlimited. Our part is to stay awake.

The Moses experience does raise the possibility that in fact God is lighting fires all around us (or leaving piles of fresh wood shavings, or speaking his word through a crowd in the church hall). He, 'Wisdom', is calling and waving but we fail to attend. We trudge on, head down, grimly determined, complaining to ourselves about our unexciting Christian life and how predictable and boring it all is, oblivious of wisdom's presence.

'Our eyes by seeing learn to see' suggests that we should not theorize about this business of looking and listening. Plunge in. Experiment. Look with faith and expectancy at the events, the people, the work ahead and pray to see what God has concealed there for you. Within the stream of impressions, sights and sounds, pray to discern 'wisdom' pulling your attention around towards this situation, or towards that person. The instances we have mentioned, especially the burning bush, are rather glamorous and quote-worthy examples of what God is doing all the time within our ordinariness. Emily Dickinson said, 'Not revelation it is that waits, but our unfurnished eyes.'

This is a creative way to live in which our Creator-Lord draws our lives into spiritual fruitfulness while allowing us to be wholly ourselves – in fact, never more ourselves then when responding to his will within the flow of daily life. Of course we are very seldom aware of it at the time. We live by faith that what we do each day, God takes into his wider designs. Our part is to stay alert, available, obedient and with 'furnished eyes'.

CHAPTER 9

Imagination overawed

Return to that spat between father and son over a tree filled with angels (p. 11). Years later the adult William Blake saw the incident as a case of 'the fool sees not the same tree that a wise man sees'. Hard on his old parent, maybe, but undeniably true. How does the 'wise man' see? What lies behind his powers of sight?

Some people seem able to look intently at things with focused attention and commitment. We have in previous chapters come across a number of examples of what Gerard Manley Hopkins called 'looking hard' at things. He wrote that 'what you look hard at seems to look hard at you [. . .] that which is studied closely radiates back a meaning, that which is necessarily unique because each manifestation of the world is somehow different from any other'.[1] That sounds like 'wise seeing'. We feel in those words a deep respect of creation in its minute particulars.

In his journal for 18 May 1870, Hopkins wrote of 'great brilliancy and projection: the eye seemed to fall perpendicular from level to level along the trees [. . .] all things hitting the senses with double but direct instress [. . .] I do not think I have ever seen anything more beautiful than the bluebell I have been looking at. I know the beauty of our Lord by it.'[2] His remarks encourage us to come closer and to take more seriously (joyfully seriously) the things we observe, and to esteem them as God's gift.

Thomas Traherne, too, experienced ecstatic joy in observing life. He tells us to delight in our calling as 'heirs to the world'.

In one of his best-known passages in his meditations he unfolds his vision:

> [Y]ou never enjoy the world aright, till the sea itself floweth in your veins, till you are clothed with the heavens, and crowned with the stars; and perceive yourself to be the sole heir of the whole world: and more then so, because men are in it who are everyone sole heirs, as well as you. Till you can sing and rejoice and delight in God, as misers do in gold, and kings in sceptres, you never enjoy the world.[3]

Traherne's thoughts seem rooted in the apostle Paul's ecstatic vision of a creation destined for rebirth, when 'the creation itself will be liberated from its bondage to decay and brought into the glorious freedom of the children of God' (Romans 8.21). This suggests a second characteristic of truly 'wise seeing': the revelatory power of scripture informing the imagination.

Blake's thought world was soaked in the Bible. One early biographer wrote that 'the scriptures overawed his imagination', which is very much more than simply knowing a lot about the Bible. The purpose of reading the scriptures is first to look at them, and then to look through them.

If, for example, you wear spectacles to read this page you do not look at your lenses, you look through them. Scripture is the lens through which the world comes into focus.

Scripture reveals Christ to be the Logos of God, the Word who speaks all creation into existence and holds it in being and form: 'All things are held together in him [. . .] he is the radiance of God's glory, the stamp of God's very being, and he sustains the universe by his word of power' (Colossians 1.17; Hebrews 1.3; cf. John 1.1–3). An imagination 'overawed' by such a revelation will certainly reject the false dualisms – spiritual/material, religion/science, God/world – which divide God from his creation. Hence Blake's vision of the God of the atom, in his poem 'Auguries of Innocence':

> To see a world in a grain of sand
> And Heaven in a wild flower,
> Hold infinity in the palm of your hand
> And eternity in an hour . . .

That is not a romantic, tree-hugging, nature-worshipping pantheism which sees Christ contained in everything. It is, rather, Christocentric 'pan*en*theism', Christ upholding everything. Only a truly biblical view of the world could celebrate a grain of sand in such a way.

By scripture informing our imaginations we find ourselves looking with bifocal vision. The first focus is the natural, near, camera image. The second focus, which occurs at the same moment as the first, sees the same object in terms of its value, meaning and purpose within the will of God. The two images are superimposed by bifocal vision on to one another to make a unified picture. Thus the prophet Isaiah looked at the city of Jerusalem, the real, solid, historical city, for what it was. That was the first focus, the natural image which any camera would register. But even as he looked, under the illumination of the Holy Spirit, the natural Jerusalem dissolved, blurred, and emerged as a world-city, the world-temple, the world-school of peace for the nations (Isaiah 2.1–5). That second, prophetic focus sees the embattled, backsliding, compromised Jerusalem for what it could and will be by the transforming power and grace of God. Bifocal sight is prophetic sight.

To refer to Blake once more, he looked at the dirty bricks and mortar of his beloved London and saw them for what they were, dirty bricks and mortar. There was nothing dreamy in his scathing attacks on the grim realities of London life forced on the new masses coming into the city. That was his first focus; a real, instinctive, camera shot of the place. But as he looked at those physical realities he saw emerging a city of angels and prophets, the city it might yet become within the purposes of God's grace. A biblical city.

The scriptures filled Blake's inner world with a vast vocabulary of events, images, symbols, words, which gave him an alternative way of seeing. He knew the city-visions in Isaiah and Ezekiel and their full realization in the Book of Revelation. He experienced what Austin Farrer termed 'a rebirth of images' as the ancient texts worked in fresh ways in his mind for reinterpretations of the present world.

Blake's vision of England was also bifocal. At one level he railed against the social and natural devastation brought by the new machine age with its infamous 'dark satanic mills' (except the 'mills' in question were not those in Bradford or Huddersfield, but were a metaphor for the new materialistic philosophy of 'progress'). That was Blake's first focus of England, obvious to everyone, not only to a visionary genius. The second focus came to him through Nehemiah's heroic work of reconstruction on shattered Jerusalem, sword in one hand and trowel in the other. Blake could not look at the brutalized land without his imagination superimposing on to it the biblical picture of a restored community. In his bifocal prophetic vision the two images merged into one 'Jerusalem'.

Another visionary whose imagination was permeated with scripture was John Bunyan. In *Grace Abounding* he describes his fellow human beings as shining 'like people that carried the broad seal of heaven about them' (an image from Revelation 7.1–4 and Ephesians 1.13, 14). The best cameras in the world will never catch that quality in people. Only the illuminating revelation of scripture will do it and provide the words and images with which to see and to describe what are otherwise commonplace things. The camera image is of course 'true'. The image mediated through scripture is even more true; the truest truth because it puts things in relation to God.

We have said that bifocal sight is prophetic sight but it is not the exclusive gift of prophets. To some extent at least all Spirit-filled people have the gift of seeing the world through scripture, although prophets have it to a greater power. Thus a

Christian cannot look at a loaf of bread without seeing it not only for what it is, a loaf, but also as having eucharistic, sacramental potential. And we look at every laughing, playful, helpless child in the light of Jesus' words. The mysterious enchanted life of a vulnerable child holds the secret to the kingdom of God (Matthew 19.13–15).

Scripture vitalizes and educates the imagination. Hence God's self-disclosure to Moses as 'I am who I am' transforms the way we look at the future (Exodus 3.14). Scholars suggest the root meaning of that divine name is something like 'I will become with you' or 'I am who I am, I will be who I will be'. He is the God who reveals himself in ways which fit each situation as it arises. He is the God who is already ahead, ready to welcome us into the future which belongs to him. When you get there you will find God to be everything you require him to be in that circumstance.

He eludes our grasp and our need to pin him down to patterns we can master and manipulate for our own ends. But when the 'imagination is overawed' by the knowledge of God as 'I will become with you' we then abandon our neat theories about how God should work. This can be a disturbing idea. It may reveal how rigid and programmatic our God-imagination has become under the steady pressure of secularism, and how limited and falsely rationalistic our 'vision' in fact is. With the young Blake's tree of angels still in mind, let me give a personal experience.

We were attending a mission conference in Manila. On a free afternoon, several of our group visited the notorious municipal rubbish mountain which is home to some of Manila's poorest. They live on that huge mass of garbage, and live off it by reclaiming stuff to use or for selling on. One of our group, a well-known biblical scholar, who visited that appalling place told us later what happened to him. He had been so distressed by the spectacle that he cried. As he was standing there in tears he became aware of numbers of 'resident' children gathering around him trying to comfort him. He said: 'But when I looked at the children what I saw were angels, beautiful, glowing, smiling angels concerned for me in my distress.'

The reaction of those of us who had not visited the mountain was interesting. Frankly embarrassed by his account, and not at all sure how we ought to respond to the idea of young angels on a rubbish tip, we suggested an alternative explanation of the experience. We told our friend that he had been greatly upset; the sun was shining low and into his eyes which could not focus properly because of his tears. This, then, would account for the shimmering glow he saw (or thought he saw) around those children. A perfectly reasonable aberration in the circumstances, we suggested.

But he would have none of it and accused us of being at heart a bunch of old-fashioned, unreconstructed rationalists, embarrassed and destabilized by the freedom in which God reveals himself to people. His own faith and imagination were informed by the scriptures which tell of people encountering 'angels without knowing it' (Hebrews 13.2); and 'are not all angels ministering spirits sent to serve those who will inherit salvation?' (Hebrews 1.14) The three who 'ministered' to Abraham and Sarah (Genesis 18.1–15) appeared as 'three men standing nearby' with not a wing or feather to show between them. Our field of spiritual vision is far too boxed in by our stubborn underlying secularism. That episode on the rubbish mountain in Manila is surely a case of 'the fool sees not the same angels as a wise man sees'.

This meditation is taking us rapidly out of our depth! But scripture has that effect when we allow it to 'overawe the imagination'. The Bible requires us to open up our vision to the sovereign activities of the God who cannot be tamed or confined within our 'reasonable' limits. If we baulk at the idea of child-angels on an Asian garbage dump, what are we to make of the claim that people see divine activity in the realm of dreams?

When Job complained that God was absent and silent, the young man Elihu disagreed:

> God does speak – now one way, now another –
>   though man may not perceive it.
> In a dream, in a vision of the night,
>   when deep sleep falls on men
>   as they slumber in their beds,
> he may speak in their ears
>   and terrify them with warnings [. . .]
>
> (Job 3.14–16)

Janet, who lives in a Yorkshire village, told me she was about twelve when she had a dream which she knew would be tremendously significant for her although at the time she did not know how. In her dream she saw a man standing in front of five arches. Some forty years later she moved with her husband to a new house in another part of the county. Soon after they had settled in there was a knock at the door. She opened it and immediately recognized the caller as the man in her dream so many years earlier. He was the vicar!

Under his ministry, Janet and her husband came to faith in Christ. But what about the five arches in the dream? A short time before Janet told me this remarkable story she and her husband were repairing the carpet in the chancel of their medieval village church. She needed to reach the edge of the carpet which touched the foot of the ancient stone altar. When she pulled back the altar coverings in order to do the work she saw cut into the altar a design of five arches. The man stands in front of the five arches every Sunday!

We began this chapter by wondering how the wise man sees. He, she, looks intently. And he, she, will emulate Blake's imagination, 'overawed' by scripture under the illumination of the Holy Spirit.

The effect will be that our observations of the world will be refracted through praise and worship. The impact of scripture on the imagination will mean that we see everything with a boundlessly grateful mind. Life fuels praise, and praise in turn feeds back to empower and expand eyesight and hearing. So the spiral of 'seeing–thanksgiving–seeing' climbs and deepens to involve the whole personality. This is to respond to God's call to 'choose life' (Deuteronomy 30.19).

A fascinating demonstration of a praising-vision is found in the best teachers of Judaism. Their conviction is that life is a flow of God's goodness, one blessing after another. Expect it, and look for it. 'Blessing God' gives routine expression to that conviction even when life is tough. Indeed, praise may be the only way to survive certain grim experiences. Judaism has special phrases by which to bless a sacred book, the washing of hands, the food they eat, the sight of the moon, the fact that they are not slaves, and that the rooster can tell night from day. They bless dwarfs, and trees in first blossom. They bless the hearing of good news and any kind of wine. Or more precisely, they bless the Holy One who stands within and behind them all. There is also a thanksgiving which runs, 'Blessed are You, O Lord [. . .] who has not made me a Rabbi.'

'Blessings', writes a Rabbi, 'keep our awareness of life's holy potential ever present. They awaken us to our own lives. Every blessing uttered extends the boundaries of the sacred and reclaims life from the deadly realm of secularism. Everywhere we turn, everything we touch, everyone we see.'[4]

That thrilling vision suggests an imagination overawed by the knowledge that:

> Holy, holy, holy is the Lord Almighty;
> the whole earth is full of his glory.
>
> (Isaiah 6.3)

Hearing comes first and makes seeing possible. The word tells me what to look for and what is a corresponding answer. In scripture it is the hearing, the hearing above all that makes us truly human. Now we must explore further how to hear God speak; to listen in such a way that possibly our imaginations will be overawed by the word.

CHAPTER 10

Listening for God

꽃 꽃 꽃

'Don't slit open the skylark to look for the song' is excellent
advice both for the protection of wild birds and for listening
to God in scripture. The living God speaks living words
through the ancient words of the Bible, but it matters how
we listen for his voice. Perhaps you, too, have sat under a kind
of painstaking exegetical preaching which analyses the text
into small bits 'to look for the song' (George Herbert called
it 'crumbing the bread'). Everything is explained but in the
end we are left strangely unmoved. We return home more
informed about the languages, customs, cultures and political
context of the biblical world, but with no word from God for
us today ringing in our ears. Technical, academic knowledge
of a bird's anatomy will never make it sing.

Do not misunderstand what I am saying here. We need all
the help we can get from good scholarship in order to understand the words of scripture. God speaks through known
grammars, verbs and tenses and by words which change
meanings over time. Biblical experts who are able to unravel
and interpret to us the ancient world are God's gift to his
Church. Our ministers complete expensive theological training
in order to emerge equipped to teach the meaning of scripture
to their congregations.

Eugene Peterson writes that 'the exegetically careless pastor
should be sued, if there were a way of doing it, with the same
diligence and on the same grounds as the surgeon who uses a
septic scalpel'.[1] Yes, but the scalpel analogy cuts both ways. If
you must use a scalpel, first anaesthetize your patient. But

chloroformed songbirds do not sing very well. Neither will we hear the Lord's voice in scripture if we come at it in a masterful surgeon-like manner, analytical scalpel in hand, set on making God's word talk to us.

We believe scripture to be what it claims to be, revelation, a written representation of God's decisive action in the creation and redemption of his world, conveyed to chosen human beings by the inspiration of the Holy Spirit. But for God's here-and-now word to come, oven-fresh, through the ancient scriptures something else must happen. A change of name provides a clue to what that essential 'something' is.

For many years an international Bible-reading agency published materials entitled *Daily Notes* to help readers understand a Bible passage each day. Gradual feedback from their public led them to change the name from *Daily Notes* to *Encounter with God*. It was very much more than a cosmetic move for marketing purposes. 'Notes' suggests the jottings we bring away from lectures; a gathering of Bible knowledge. 'Notes' suggests an attempt to slit open the skylark to find the song. Readers were telling the publishers that they were looking for more when they turned to the Bible.

Encounter with God suggests that there is indeed much more going on when we read scripture than simply the transference of knowledge from the page into the reader's brain. 'Encounter' is a meeting, an engagement between minds and hearts in which surprising transactions are possible. And an 'encounter with God' is what we want. What will allow it to happen?

First, our *attitude*. The primary reason for taking scripture seriously is that Jesus made it the test and the proof of our love for him. 'If anyone loves me, he will obey my teaching [. . .] My Father will love him, and we will come to him and make our home with him' (John 14.23). It is the supreme encounter. Attention to scripture promises not just words about God, but the life and fellowship of God with us. If the Father and Son 'make their home with you' in the power of the Holy Spirit conversation will flow. Why else would great people choose to move in with those who love them, if not to eat and to talk together?

Second, if we take seriously the invitation to hear the Lord in and through scripture some *discipline of preparation* is necessary. Millions of Christians over the years have used versions of an approach associated with Scripture Union. There are five steps:

- **Focus** – Spend some moments in silence to bring together your scattered attention on what is about to happen. The Lord is here. You stand on holy ground.
- **Pray** – Ask the Lord and author of scripture to reveal himself as you read and meditate on his word. Confess your sins and ask for a cleansed mind attuned by the Holy Spirit to discern the voice of the Lord.
- **Read** – Take your chosen passage of scripture. Read it through at normal speed, and then again verse by verse using aids to clarify obscure or difficult phrases.
- **Reflect** – Certain verses or ideas will have emerged as particularly significant for you. Stay with them, or choose one of them. Walk around it in your mind. Turn it over and over as you think about it; mix in your longings; allow your thoughts to develop into a conversation with God. Listen to what is coming through to you from the Holy Spirit of scripture, 'the interior master'.
- **Pray** – In response to what you are hearing, breathe back to God your thanksgiving and requests for power to obey his word. Allow your meditation to fuel your intercession for others.

Of the five stages mentioned, the one which holds the key to an 'encounter' with God is also the one which is most elusive: *reflection*. It is a discipline which runs counter to the way we are today. We quite soon learn the knack of grasping the gist of a passage, but that could be little better than slitting open the songbird. Thoughts which stay on top of the brain come to nothing, as Jesus once famously explained (Matthew 13.4, 19). Reflection, meditation, contemplation, refers to the process of opening up our inner life to receive the word of scripture at deeper levels. Within the heart and the imagination conversation with Father and Son is possible.

We cannot force the process (which is why it is so irksome to the modern mind). 'Soak and wait' is sound advice. Take the analogy of the jeweller tumble-polishing semi-precious stones. Into a small drum he places the stones to be polished along with a thin paste of fine carborundum grit. The drum is switched on and the stones mixed with the paste trundle around together for hours. The action of the grit on the stones produces a smooth, polished, beautiful surface. It takes time – trust the process.

Reflection is something like tumble-polishing. We allow our thoughts (the stones) to rub against the polishing grit (scripture) as they turn over and over with no time limit. Here is an example:

Let us say that our reading for the day is Luke 12.1–21. We follow our steps for preparation: focus, prayer, read. It is a high-voltage passage about the opposition Christ's people can expect in the world. It is about making up our minds to be faithful to him before those who criticise the faith, and in the practical decisions of daily life. This is all relevant, and as we read, our own situation starts to take shape around Christ's words and we feel he is speaking not only to a first-century audience but to us also.

As we read, weighing and pondering the words, soaking our minds in them, a couple of verses seem to stand out. They reach out to us. They speak to our innate nervousness about being known as an uncompromising Christian where we work. In verses 6–7, Jesus says, 'Are not five sparrows sold for two pennies? Yet not one of them is forgotten by God. Indeed, the very hairs of your head are all numbered. Don't be afraid; you are worth more than many sparrows.'

We feel these words are a wonderful encouragement to trust God for the outcome of our lives when we commit ourselves to him. But an anxiety persists. Does God *really* know and care about the small details of our daily life? We turn to the exegetical help – material of the *Encounter with God* type, or perhaps a commentary on Luke. There an expert in the background to the New Testament points out that the Rabbis in Jesus' day taught that God was so busy running the universe that when people pray, they should not bother him with requests 'smaller than a bird's nest'.

Now verses 6 and 7 are becoming very interesting. Jesus used the sparrow metaphor to reject the Rabbis' teaching. He was saying, 'How wrong you are. A bird's nest? Why, even a tiny sparrow in the nest is kept in the Father's mind! Nothing is too small or insignificant to bring to him in prayer. If it is big enough to worry you, it is big enough to concern God.' We have a sense of breakthrough, of touching the Father's heart, of his unlimited practical interest in the small affairs of our lives. Even as we look at the squiggles on the paper at verses 6 and 7, we can, as it were, see and hear the Lord coming through to embrace the whole of our lives for this day.

Now our thoughts are in the tumble-polisher with Christ's words, turning over and over, changing shape and texture. Some, we can see, are already shining. We concentrate on those and pursue our meditation with them, mixed with prayer, confession, praise, petition. At the end of our time of meditation and reflection, the tumble-polisher is still on, slowly turning over and over, quite without our conscious effort. At one or two unoccupied moments throughout the day we will stop the drum and inspect the thought-stones to see how things are developing. We might even buy ourselves a convenient notebook to jot down some of the meditations.

Thus the ancient word of God becomes the place where we meet him and discern his living word for here and now.

You can by now guess the next possible step in our encounter with God in scripture. It is to furnish our inner world with his word, even to recover the defunct discipline of memorizing scripture. Luke 12.6–7, for example, would take a few minutes at most to memorize yet it would then become a living focus for meditative reflection. Why should we allow the inconsequential rubbish of the wall-to-wall entertainment and advertising which permeate our daily life to stuff their images into our minds? Surely we are responsible for seeing that it does not happen by taking the initiative through memorizing scripture. 'I have hidden your word in my heart that I might not sin against you' (Psalm 119.11). That is to say, God's word has power to create and impart what it desires to see in us.

When we allow God to take up his presence within our minds by his word, we discover that the scriptures exert their unique power and light; we experience them as Wallace Stevens did poetry, as 'a violence from within that protects us from the violence from without'.[2] Take responsibility for the state of your inner life. The scriptures through which God dwells within us and speaks with us fuel the violence of God's grace which pushes back against the corrupting, dark 'violence from without'.

If we love God we will want to hold his word deep in the memory where insight will lead to an abiding consciousness of his presence. It is something like carrying a photo of a loved one in your memory, except it is experienced as a living presence. The word of God in the heart creates a change of climate: it alters the inner weather of our psychological world so that new plantings of the Spirit can flourish, reshaping the landscape of the mind.

The word of Christ held within the memory acts like a

pace-maker at the centre of our inner life. George Steiner writes about memorizing:

> [T]o learn by heart is to afford the text or music an indwelling clarity and life-force [. . .] What we know by heart becomes an agency in our consciousness, a 'pace-maker' in the growth and vital complication of our identity [. . .] Accurate recollection and resort in remembrance not only deepen our grasp of the work: they generate a shaping reciprocity between ourselves and that which the heart knows.

And he continues in praise of the memorized word, '[W]hat matters even more, it safeguards the core of individuality.'[3]

Thus we are given a picture of God speaking his word at the centre of our lives, setting up its healing and vitalizing rhythms throughout our imaginative thought world. Our meditation and prayer will then not simply float dreamily away but be rooted in, and nourished by, the remembered word. And the Lord will appear in the inner room of the mind.

CHAPTER 11

Different readings

༜ ༜ ༜

We read people when we observe them. Simone Weil said, 'Everyone cries out to be read differently.' We feel as our deepest instinct that we possess an inner core of individuality different from others. We seem to have arrived in this world carrying a sort of message which is encoded in our body, mind, mannerisms, temperament, personality. These are things we hardly dare say outside of a few trusted friends; it sounds pompous to talk of our having a special meaning, but the conviction persists in our deepest heart. Society is inclined to dismiss such ideas as so much romanticism. 'There are seven billion people crammed on to this planet and you want to be different!'

But who is there sufficiently interested and perceptive enough to come close and read the strange hieroglyphs across our individuality? *This constitutes the greatest challenge to the way we observe other people.* No one actually parades with a placard saying 'Read me differently'. Not in so many words. But Christians should be known for their sensitivity to the cry for recognition implicit in much that goes on in society. In fact we have here a fair definition of the Christian's ministry in the world, for we are named after Christ, the Lord of the individual, who left the ninety-nine to go in search of the one.

Here we are concerned with individuality, not with individualism. Individualism, as a life-style, manifests itself as a rampant, self-centred thrust towards unlimited choice with fewer and fewer personal boundaries imposed from without. As such it is the engine which drives our consumerist culture.

It would be hypocritical to deny that it produces enormous material benefits, for some, but as an answer to our question, 'Who can tell me my difference?', it is a shallow deception. Hence the pervasive sense of our being busy but bored, satiated yet still restless and frustrated. We should not be surprised at the flight into all kinds of 'I-me-myself' cults and the proliferation of 'self-enhancement' programmes.

It seems that Isaiah's picture was surely recorded as much for our time as for his:

> [. . .] as it is with a dream,
>   with a vision in the night –
> as when a hungry man dreams that he is eating,
>   but he awakens, and his hunger remains;
> as when a thirsty man dreams that he is drinking,
>   but he awakens faint, with his thirst unquenched [. . .]
>   (Isaiah 29.7–8)

Individualism is a dream, a teasing image. It can feed many of our superficial needs, but never reveals our personal meaning. Perhaps one reason why we are so fascinated with space exploration at the present time is that we can understand a star on the far side of the galaxy more easily than we can know our inner selfhood. W. B. Yeats described his 'heart' as:

> Sick with desire
> And fastened to a dying animal
> It knows not what it is.[1]

Looking and listening will therefore include being aware of the complex signals given out by people indicating their hopes to be taken seriously, and read intelligently, and valued for their unique difference.

Hang-gliding off the north face of the Eiger used to be an impressive statement of an individual's exceptional qualities. Until everyone else caught up with it and now Swiss children do it before breakfast. The rest of us may settle for the less spectacular and more comfortable line of joining a club, or choosing a particular pub, or attending this church instead of that one even though it is closer, all with the hope of recognition, of being accepted and valued if only by a few. And should we fail to get to a gathering it can be strangely uplifting to learn later that 'we missed you'.

My wife (the same wife who pointed out the owls in chapter 5) once spent a summer in the Scottish Borders cleaning and reopening defunct mission halls in some of the villages. Her stories from that time entered our family folklore and when some 24 years later we were driving up to Edinburgh, I suggested we make a detour to visit Kirk Yetholme, where Sonja was based during her couple of months' work. We found the mission hall in the village, just as she had described. This was the place she had scrubbed out and where she started up children's activities. Here also she had given her first-ever public talk in English (Sonja is Swiss), although halfway through her presentation a child rushed in and the wind blew her notes everywhere. I wanted to see inside.

The hall appeared in working order but locked. A local pointed out to us the house where the key was kept. In the Scottish good-weather fashion the door was open, so I knocked, wondering how I would start to explain to the key-holder this story about a young Swiss woman who had stayed briefly in the village a quarter of a century ago. An elderly woman came slowly to the door and, without a moment's hesitation and with no indication of anything unusual, looked at my wife and said, 'Why, it's Sonja!' It is, believe me, very wonderful to be known and remembered. It answers to something very deep within us.

For a more in-your-face claim to distinctiveness note the practice of tattooing; or metal studs pierced into sensitive flesh; or startling hairstyles and bizarre clothes. They say, 'Look! Don't ignore me. This is what I am and I'm not a bit like you.' Again, there is the practice of issuing 'personal mission statements', as if to say, 'This is my life and I know where I am going.' Or again, there are people who take themselves so very seriously that they compose their own obituary (beforehand), presumably because no others, not even close relatives or friends, can be trusted to honour the remarkable qualities of the deceased. Also inspired, at least in part, by the need to be remembered and 'experienced' after death, is the practice of drafting 'the letter I would write to my child on the day I die'. The whole vast complex of memorial–commemorative–thanksgiving events across the world, year after year, testifies to our longing to have been thought significant in our lifetime.

These are instances of our determination to prove Shakespeare wrong in his pessimistic view of our existence:

> Life's but a walking shadow, a poor player
> That struts and frets his hour upon the stage,
> And then is heard no more . . .

We are looking and listening for something of profound significance coming up out of the deep heart of our neighbour; and once more we discover that what we require for the task is not a technique but an attitude.

Before we turn to Jesus Christ who alone can decipher the hieroglyphs of individuality, it may help at this point just to note three terms used by Gerard Manley Hopkins, he who saw life as 'all things counter, original, spare, strange' (p. 28), and who discovered that what you look hard at looks hard back at you. In his deeply orthodox vision individuation is the characteristic of creation. Everyone and everything has its own unique 'this-ness' unlike anything else.

Hopkins coined the term 'inscape'. We speak of landscape and seascape; 'inscape', one Hopkins scholar has written, 'is not a superficial appearance; rather it is the expression of the inner core of individuality, perceived in moments of insight by an onlooker who is in full harmony with the being he is observing'.[2] Hopkins' way of looking into creation was to stand open before it, teachable and receptive, 'in full harmony' with it, ready to come under the impression of its inscape. Every movement, action and effort reveals something of a unique inner self-hood. Which is to say that Hopkins mimicked the divine way of observation: 'The Lord does not look at the things man looks at. Man looks at the outward appearance, but the Lord looks at the heart' (1 Samuel 16.7). God searches for our inscape.

Hopkins used a second term to describe the way the observer experiences an inscape. He called it 'selving'. The object we are looking at 'selves', its essential self and inscape coming out to you in revelation. The self is known by the act of being true to its nature, 'selving'. Thus the kingfisher is selving when it flashes past like a small burst of flame and you glimpse its 'kingfisherness'. But a bell also 'selves' when it rings: it 'flings out' its name, says Hopkins (see his poem 'As Kingfishers Catch Fire . . .'). Everything and everyone deals out, from its essential store of unique individuality, its self, 'crying *what I do is me: for that I came . . .*'.

Properly esteemed, all people and all things are released from the warping pressure of false competitiveness. All that matters is that each self (your-self, my-self, his-self) plays its part in the cosmic thanksgiving to God. John of the Cross wrote: 'All creatures tell, in their own language, what God is in them, and their voices together make up a wonderful song. It is a silent music because it communicates a soft tranquil sensation, untroubled by human voices, and simultaneously affords the enjoyment of sounds and the peace of silence.'

In the Lake District Hopkins recorded in his journal for one morning: 'Hard frost, bright sun, a sky of blue water [. . .] ground sheeted with taut tattered streaks of crisp gritty snow [. . .] I saw the inscape though freshly, as if my eye were still growing.'[3] Thus this profoundly gifted observer suggests that the inner self of the thing we are looking at, its inscape, may not explode in the eye instantaneously, but may require more prolonged and contemplative observation with our eye 'still growing'. Earlier we referred to this sense of our powers of perception expanding and strengthening as 'my eye by seeing learns to see'. Analytical scrutiny it certainly is not, more like finding the song by allowing the skylark to sing.

Another journal entry: 'A beautiful instance of inscape [. . .] is seen in the behaviour of the flag flower from the shut bud to the full blowing.'[4] A flower selving, revealing its selfhood by being itself in blooming. Again, when looking down over a garden in the moonlight: 'The moon just marked by a blue spot pushing its way through the dark cloud [. . .] the garden with the heads of the trees and shrubs furry grey: I read a broad careless inscape flowing throughout.'[5]

Looking for the inscape, the essence of individuality in a person, Hopkins employed a third term: 'the burl of being'. The burl is an old word for the knot in a piece of wood and the tangled tight mass in sheep's wool. Applied to a person, the 'burl of being' is the tightly grained, dense, impenetrable concentration in the personality, a characteristic of individuality. It is quirkiness, bias, force, strength, for better or for worse. It is your 'self' or my 'self'. God does not discard the piece of wood because of its awkward burl, neither does he smash the knot, but works with it. Christ was a man like us, and knows from the inside all about the burl of being. He reveals the wisdom of his experiential knowledge by bending and shaping his own power to follow the direction of the grain of our burl. He can incorporate the burl so that in the end that awkward, stubborn knot appears indispensable to the design of the finished piece. To Peter, he said 'You are . . . you shall be'.

Inscape – selving – burl are all reflected in looks, gesture, language, actions, choices, attitudes. The key is with ourselves, the observer; 'the insight of the onlooker who is in full harmony with the being he is observing' is a spiritual attitude before it is an artistic one. It requires a cleansed life and a mind habitually under the inspiration of the Holy Spirit. The

only way I know by which to attain anything like 'full harmony'
with the 'being' I am observing is to look at it prayerfully.
Try it. The difference is immediately apparent. People or situations are different when prayed for, or rather we see them
another way. Pray in your heart and mind for that person over
there and they will appear to you differently, more real. To
adapt Blake's saying once more, 'The prayerless man sees not
the same world that the prayerful man sees.'

Earlier we called Jesus the Lord of the individual. He alone
is able to answer our desire to be read differently, known for
what and who we are. More exactly he is the Lord of his new
community composed of people who are finding their true
difference in him. Jesus stood at the focus of that movement
throughout the Old Testament period in which men and
women gradually discovered their individuality, culminating in
the promise of a new covenant, and a new place for 'self-hood',
given through the prophet Jeremiah:

> 'This is the covenant that I will make with the house of Israel
>   after that time,' declares the Lord.
> 'I will put my law in their minds
>   and write it on their hearts.
> I will be their God,
>   and they will be my people.
> No longer will a man teach his neighbour,
>   or a man his brother, saying, "Know the Lord,"
> because they will all know me,
>   from the least of them to the greatest,'
> declares the Lord.

(Jeremiah 31.33–4)

That was an astonishing promise of authentic individuality
which Christ the mediator of the new covenant came to inau-
gurate. This new kind of individual, in a new relationship
with God by the Holy Spirit, is delivered from the constraints
of the collective and free from the oppressive coercive power

of tradition. But notice very carefully in what true individuality consists: the call of God.

In other words that which tells me my unique difference is not to be found within me. Sift through my DNA and any other readings of who I am and you will *not* find that elusive, unique difference to read it. It lies outside, in God, and must be received from him in his call, 'I am the Lord, the God of Israel, who summons you by name' (Isaiah 45.3). You become your true self when you hear God call your name, when you are summoned by his voice; addressed by his will; invited by his love; possessed by his Holy Spirit. Thus you are called into life and your true, unique, inner self-hood flourishes.

Therefore, however conscientiously we look at and listen to other people 'to read them differently', it must be in relation to the call of God. We assume that the Lord is calling them in his mysterious ways, which it is not our business to know. Jesus said, 'Come to me, all you who are weary and burdened, and I will give you rest' (Matthew 11.28). That is the call. Only within his rest can our inner selves flourish. Therefore, should a friend ask the great question 'Who am I?' (or words to that effect) our answer will include the essential ingredient – the call of God, for which your inner self is waiting, like an echo chamber. It is the call to freedom, to meaning, to participation in God's purposes. It is the call to Christ and into the company of true individuals, the people of the new covenant.

We said at the start of this chapter that the Christian will want to be sensitive to that 'cry to be read differently' however it appears among the people we meet. Not just to see and hear it, of course, but in order to respond as best we can. We cannot ourselves remain disengaged observers at arm's length from people who are seeking self-understanding. If we share with them the news that a person discovers their authentic individuality by hearing and responding to the call of God, we will be inescapably involved in personal testimony.

Our friend will want to know what 'the call' is, what the

voice of God might sound like, and how we ourselves experienced the call of that beautiful voice and what difference it has made to us since.

For your meditation take the story of the man born blind, in John chapter 9. He describes the contours of our own lives: personal blindness; the call of the Christ who is 'the light of the world' (v. 5); restored sight; then his testimony, 'One thing I do know. I was blind but now I see' (v. 25); faith and worship (vv. 35–8); and notice how his new life is a witness, and possibly also an offence, to others.

CHAPTER 12

Memory-sight

✣ ✣ ✣

Memory is essential for true sightedness. Memory feeds insight – amnesia works myopia. That truth runs like an organizing spine through scripture. If you want to look into the future, keep in vital touch with your spiritual origins. In fact the scriptures are our essential memory written down. Without it we would be walled in by the present which then assumes absolute value; we would then take the here and now far too seriously since we would have nothing to test it by. That is our claim for the memory-sight which is the theme for this chapter. Not everyone agrees with it! The star of the L'Oreal TV advertisement for one. She pours her elegant scorn on certain cosmetics because 'they are so . . . *yesterday*'.

It is an article of faith for our culture that any connection with 'yesterday' and its works is the unforgivable sin. Similarly, it has been known for one politician to damn another politician in the nicest possible way as being 'yesterday's man'. The message could not be more plain. According to the prevailing wisdom progressive people have no dealings with the past. The past is a spent commodity, suitable for museums and archives of nostalgia which have a section entitled 'Where are they now?' The future awaits those who can jettison the dead-weight of yesterday (though you can keep your record of the charming Beatles' song of that name). Connections with what used to be could seriously damage the health of your image as a forward-looking individual. The past, so runs this idea, has nothing for us as we look towards a future unimaginably different from anything seen so far. Homo-up-to-date-um reigns!

The point we are making is this: only as our looking and listening are suffused with those awesome memories deep in the tradition of God's people, of God's decisive, miraculous self-revelation in deed and word, recorded in scripture, will we ever be able to perceive the future – and then to re-perceive it for what it could be under the God of resurrection. Truly creative and original perceptions of the future, in which we imagine the unimaginable, will arise out of those immense, elemental memories. We for our part must meditate, pray and think with the scriptures open before us in order to stay in vital communion with those decisive memories.

In his book *The Making of Memory* Steven Rose writes: 'Memory defines who we are and shapes the way we act more closely than any other single aspect of our personhood. All of life is a trajectory from experience past to unknown future.'[1] A condition such as Alzheimer's Disease seems therefore a catastrophe, for the loved ones as well as for the sufferer who they witness slipping away from them as memory disintegrates and with it the loved personality.

We fight for certain memories, and resist expressions of social amnesia by groups who seek to organize forgetting. Shameful acts in a war come to mind. Hence we work to maintain the memory of the Holocaust because, we believe, it was a manifestation of something appalling embedded deep in the human family which travels with the race. Similarly, in the former Soviet Union, the society set up to commemorate the victims of the Stalin era is known as 'Memorial'. Some things we must remember never to forget if we are ever to steer a path into the future. Asia and Africa have endured their 'Holocaust' atrocities also, while back in Europe the Kosovo horrors are one recent endorsement of Pascal's opinion that 'man is the glory and the scum of the universe'. Christians will not be surprised at these serial incarnations of evil. Shocked, yes, but not surprised, since our biblical memory includes the story of primordial 'Holocaust' disorders in creation and the Fall (Genesis 1—3).

We are educated to look at human behaviour, and behind the behaviour to its source in the heart, through the memory of Adam displacing God when he raided the 'tree of the knowledge of good and evil'. From the outset humankind claimed authority to choose what is right and wrong, good and evil, life and death, as the angels looked on in horror. We are therefore not surprised at personal, social or international chaos. We are incorrigible sinners. 'Sin is crouching at your door; it desires to have you, but you must master it' (Genesis 4.7).

No one who has that first story active in their memory will ever make the mistake of taking seriously man's ludicrous pretensions to autonomy. But it is only through such memories as an informing presence in our lives that we are able to look into the future realistically yet with expectation. A young Israeli tour guide was showing our group around the ruins of the fortress at Masada where Jewish resistance fighters were slaughtered in their final stand against the Roman army of occupation in AD 74. He concluded his account of the tragedy with a vehement promise, 'Never again!' Masada, with the Holocaust, is a national memory which gives present-day Israelis their distinctive stance in relation to the future.

We must receive and cultivate seminal biblical memories in ways scripture prescribes. It is not enough just to know about them, or where to find them in the Bible. Have them in your heart, and 'by heart'. That which is known by heart is what the heart knows. Memory will lead to insight which will lead to permanent consciousness. It will re-form and in-form your mind and heart and create a tone, a colour, an atmosphere, which affects the way you attend to things, your sight and hearing. When Deuteronomy 6.6 charges that 'these commandments that I give you today are to be upon your hearts', it means that the hearer should remain conscious of them. It is, therefore, an encounter with those memories that is required, in which God's word is constantly present to the mind and thence into the store of vital memory-wisdom (look again at the stones in the tumble-polisher illustration in chapter 10).

> Keep my commands and you will live;
>> guard my teachings as the apple of your eye.
> Bind them on your fingers;
>> write them on the tablet of your heart.
>
> (Proverbs 7.2–3)

To keep God's word 'in your heart' means in your memory.

Notice once more the order of things. First listening (reading) and attending to God's word, receiving it into our heart-memory. Thus we become empowered and advised by our memories to see as God sees. And all the time this process is going on other powers are active to subvert our concentration and to induce amnesia. Paul refers to them as 'the powers and authorities', spiritual powers which work through, and at times even possess, certain concentrations of human mind and energies. Their aim is to create and orchestrate a sustained forgetting of Christian memories and thereby to darken our vision of the way ahead.

We are able to draw together the various strands of this meditation by visiting Israel in Babylonian exile. Christians have always seen the Babylonian captivity as the paradigm of the Church in the world.

The situation was as follows: after a long and dismal period of disobedience towards God, he allowed Israel to fall under the sway of the Babylonian empire in 597 BC. Many prominent Israelite families were transported north to begin a 70-year exile. It was of course an utter catastrophe for Israel, a total contradiction of everything they always believed about their favoured status as God's chosen people.

Some time into the captivity the prophet Isaiah communicated a number of messages to the exiles, included in the Book of Isaiah, chapters 40—55. He called upon the people to prepare for return by practising what have been called 'disciplines of readiness'. God has not abandoned them. He is faithful and will bring his people home to Israel and Jerusalem. The relevance of their situation in exile to ourselves as the Church in this society is striking. So are Israel's 'disciplines of readiness'.

First, Israel in captivity found that her old story had ground to a halt. Our traditional story as Christ's Church in this country has similarly run out of steam. We no longer have a base of power or authority in a society which does not much care what the Church says about things. The job of the Church, it seems, is to rubber-stamp and to legitimize whatever it is society decides it wants to do, much of which contradicts our faith. Israel in Babylon understood that state of affairs.

Second, Israel was compelled by the mind-numbing catastrophe of captivity under a pagan power to radically rethink her relationship with God and with the nations. Christians, too, are in some turmoil, casting around for fresh interpretations of what it means to be God's people at this time and how to discharge our mission in the world. Like Israel in Babylon, Christians feel outnumbered and outgunned by the forces of unbelief in society.

Third, Israel's response to the Babylonian imperial power in her captivity is reflected in attitudes discernible among ourselves in the Church – two in particular:

There is the way of *assimilation*. For some of the exiles their Jewishness was too heavy a burden to sustain in that all-powerful paganism. Capitulation to Babylonian norms seemed the only way for a quiet life. After all, as far as they knew they would be resident aliens in Babylon for the rest of their days. Cut your losses and get on with life. In our own 'Babylonian' situation it is possible for Christians to quietly assimilate to the dominant materialism of our culture confined within this-world boundaries to which God appears irrelevant.

Or if assimilation is resisted, *despair* is a possible response to the overwhelming presence of rampant secularism. We can imagine a faithful Jew attending the synagogue regularly while in his heart he had long since despaired of deliverance and transformation. He would, after all, pass the great effigies of Bel and Nebo, Babylonian deities, credited with that nation's enormous success and imperial expansionism (Isaiah 46.1). By a stealthy osmosis the Jewish believer's mind would be occupied with thoughts of permanent residence in Babylon. Memories of home, Jerusalem, a future under the reign of God, would fade. Amnesia creeps over the mind.

We can recognize the same attitude of quiet despair among ourselves in the Church. Hopefully, we have not yet caved in to the secular pressures and the steady drip, drip, drip of unbelief, but many of us are joyless, defensive, dutiful, lacking dynamic hope or spiritual liveliness. We settle, at best, for a tight-lipped, rather grim, stoical resolve. We have despaired of God's renewal in our affairs.

It is into this spiritual crisis that Isaiah speaks his 'disciplines of readiness'. What is so fascinating for us, in the light of our exploration of the way memories affect vision, is his message to recover our most radical spiritual memories of the Lord's transforming power in lifeless people.

> Listen to me, you who pursue righteousness
>> and who seek the Lord:
> Look to the rock from which you were cut
>> and to the quarry from which you were hewn;
> Look to Abraham, your father,
>> and to Sarah, who gave you birth.
> When I called him he was but one,
>> and I blessed him and made him many.
>
> (Isaiah 51.1–2)

The Babylonian exiles could see no future outside the limits of the empire because they had lost touch with their most elemental, definitive memories in what God did for Abraham and Sarah. What God achieved for the strange old couple holds the key to the exiles' future.

Of course they retained some memories. We can imagine a Jewish family having a meal with Babylonian neighbours and the conversation turning to pride in the achievements of their respective nations.

The Babylonians would have plenty to boast of with their great empire. And the Jews? We can see them choosing carefully the more respectable, reasonable, establishment memories which would hopefully impress their pagan friends: the conquest of Canaan, for instance, and the founding of the Temple in Jerusalem, and the monarchy. The wise Solomon would be the sort of memory a Jew could reasonably share with sophisticated, successful pagans over dinner.

But Isaiah will have none of it. Captive believers will never be delivered by culture and sophistication any more than a dead man will be raised by a classical concert. He takes Israel back to her original, primordial, embarrassingly odd memories in the mists of old Canaan. Back to miracles, life-out-of-death exodus, manna in the desert, gifts from heaven, transformations. The exiles' present situation requires nothing less. Back to the ancestral parents, Abraham and Sarah.

Remember Abraham, Isaiah is saying, because the truth about you is bound up with that man. If you desire to look out beyond the enslaving empire to a new life reconciled with God, then look at Abraham. He was a strange, impressive man of incredible trust in God who left his known world to follow God into the unknown (Genesis 12). But remember the complete Abraham, the full unedited story, the pitiful, fearful man who pathetically betrayed his wife in order to save his own skin, and who after believing in God so wonderfully for the gift of the son who would carry the promise of a great nation, next took Hagar as a surrogate wife to produce a child, just in case. Look at the confused man, the oscillating man, a man just like ourselves.

And look at Sarah, your mother in the faith. Beautiful 'princess', but look at the whole Sarah, her barrenness, her oldness, her cynicism, her inability to receive the promise of life in the gift of Isaac, her mocking laughter. She is the mother of all of us who find it difficult to believe, who are bereft of life and vision, who have no expectancy of a new life with God outside the control of the empire.

Here is the transforming memory which blasts open a new way into the future with God. In that impotent, confused old couple, 'as good as dead' (Romans 4.19), God worked newness against all reason and evidence. You are out of that old couple, from their rock and their quarry. What God did for them in such dire and hopeless circumstances, against all possibility, he can do for you. 'I blessed him and made him many.'

Remember this radical and dangerous memory because it invites us to faith. Remember, recall, recite, embrace, celebrate, stand in solidarity with the old couple – God brought resurrection life out of their death. And remember those exiles, short on faith, assimilating to the demand of the great pagan empire, despairing of God's resurrection power. In their doubt they could not begin to visualize a change in the existing arrangements, so they compromised, capitulated, resigned themselves, accepted their appointed place within the imperial system. But then came the call to practise this discipline of dangerous, outrageous memories. The memory of their origins in Abraham and Sarah worked powerfully within the community of exiles. The memory turned them back into believers, aroused trust in the power of God to work an incredible newness in release from captivity. They recovered their faith in the impossible possibility.

Look back in order to look forward. With such irrepressible and dynamic memories we will turn and look into the future as God's future, the stage on which he works his resurrection newness. But people trapped in their amnesia, without memories, can only accept things as they appear now. It is faith-memories which connect us back with God's mighty acts among needy people like ourselves, by which we look at the world as a place where God works in ways beyond our comprehension, and beyond the limitations imposed by the world-view of 'Babylon'.

We, of course, go beyond reconnecting with Abraham and Sarah. The life-out-of-death, mighty act of God from which we are born is nothing less than the crucifixion and resurrection of our Lord Jesus Christ. In daily communion with that miracle we look at the world with new eyes.

And we sing. The sequel to Isaiah 51.1–2 is 54.1–3 where the 'barren woman' (Sarah, the exiles, the Church in this age) is invited to 'sing [. . .] burst into song, shout for joy' because of God's gift of new life in her. An extraordinary scene is suggested: smug, arrogant Babylonia will be swept aside by the outpouring of new life in 'the children of the desolate woman'.

Radical, subversive, outrageous, dangerous memories open our eyes to receive and believe equally astonishing promises concerning the restoration of an exuberant, irrepressible people of God, even though at the moment they are apparently 'barren'. It is a promise of life such as 'Babylon' can never give.

CHAPTER 13

Look as you will

ꗝ ꗝ ꗝ

So far we have considered looking and listening as our response to incoming signals. Sounds and images impinge on ear and eye. People call, life shouts, events carry messages, creation dances, the scriptures and books invite conversation, the Lord speaks. Our wisdom is to live attuned to this stream of incoming communications and to select the significant ones. But there is another, very wonderful, side to the way we observe the world. Not only do we receive; God has also set us free to transmit by looking creatively into the world.

The Lord makes and redeems us for freedom. 'If the Son sets you free, you will be free indeed' (John 8.36). Not for employment in the Heavenly Firm, but for mature freedom in the Father's family. He desires and designs that we should be free to observe, decide, initiate and act. This does not in any way threaten his status as our sovereign God; rather, it is his loving wisdom to work his purposes through our authentic freedom to choose. He delights to perform his will through our independence. The marvel of this paradox is that we are most his when most truly ourselves. And to become truly and fully ourselves we must be free to think, look, listen, and then act creatively.

It is freedom to look into the empty spaces; the lost causes; the desolate relationships; the dull, rigid, unyielding situations; to look into deathly circumstances which appear to hold no potential for joy and blessing. Free to gaze out at the wilderness and see (imagine) its transformation into a rose garden. Free, in other words, to manifest the mind of the Lord by seeing, imagining, visualizing things as yet invisible. Free to say you can see possibilities where there are none at the present; to project on to the fog images of an alternative way of seeing.

It belongs to our spiritual maturity that the Lord chooses to step aside, remove his hands, put away his lists of jobs for us to do, and ask, 'Now, tell me the best thing you can imagine when you look here.' Exercise your 'glorious freedom of the children of God' (Romans 8.21) and decide what you want to happen. It is as if God should say, 'It's a lovely day. What would you like to do? You decide and we will go and do it together.' It is that sort of freedom.

Perhaps you find this talk of freedom to imagine and initiate rather unnerving when applied to our discipleship in the kingdom of God. Disciples should do as they are told. The master does have tasks for us to fulfil. We may get confused in our freedom and mistake fantasy for true sight. Yes, we may. And we are now straying into the very important subject of metaphor and the images by which we picture God and our relationship with him. It is always futile to play the metaphors off against one another (King on his throne versus the Waiting Father). Let us just say, for now, that our bias does seem to be towards God as a director-general who trained in the Prussian School of Business Management. It is a deeply imbedded, pagan fear within our psyche that his style tends that way. The Great Production Engineer has his Five Year Plan, so jump to it.

But experience of life soon reveals that sort of notion of God as a tyranny and a deception. The most comprehensive metaphor for God's activity in the world, and in our lives in particular, is the potter working the clay. The artistic God is the source of all creativity and artistry in the world. He does not hand out an inflexible blueprint, because he is the gloriously inventive artist of light. All creation testifies to that truth. There is no right or wrong in pottery or in other artistry, only degrees of expression of ingenuity, creativity, beauty, innovation and close care. We are children of the inventive artist of light, free to look at the world through his eyes. Let us anchor this line of thought in some examples.

Take one hungry crowd of about five thousand people (John 6.1–13). Jesus handed the situation over to his disciples for their reading. He invited them to look and tell him what they saw, what they could visualize happening, how this threatening state of affairs could be saved, how so many people could be blessed and not hurt. They were free to look imaginatively but their response was merely to helplessly, cluelessly, describe a snap-shot of the situation at that moment: 'Eight months' wages would not buy enough bread for each one to have a bite' (v. 7). Practical, realistic, commonsensical – but hardly as seen through the perceptions of 'the gloriously inventive artist of light'. They looked and saw only an impossible situation.

Jesus was surely hoping for something more from them. He was not merely teasing them or playing an unkind joke on them. He wanted their imaginative, inventive interpretation, free to say how things might be changed here. In fact, Andrew glimpsed a hint of new possibility, an alternative way of reading the crisis, some potential in the boy's 'five small barley loaves and two small fish' (v. 9), a clue to divine initiatives.

If you think that is a little hard on the Lord's inner circle, turn to other examples, such as the interesting one where Jesus took a child as manifesting the character of kingdom people (Mark 10.13–16). The disciples saw children only in the usual way of that culture: as insignificant and, at that particular moment, something of a trial. Jesus is saying to them, Look! Look closely. Open your eyes, use your imagination, get beyond prevailing blind custom, see in the enchanted vulnerability of these trusting children the embodiment of everything I have been teaching you about the Family of God.

By now you will have twigged that this marvellous freedom to initiate creative looking and imagining, and to visualize transforming potential in the unlikeliest places, takes on the character of a game. A game which, like snooker for instance, has its boundaries, its rules of play, its given number and colours of balls – but having said that, the sky's the limit. Or rather the skill and ingenuity of the players is the limit. Innovate, exploit, experiment, take risks, originate as much as you will, it adds enormously to the pleasure of the game.

Or, again, the freedom within the will of God that we are exploring may be compared to music. Think of the will of God for your life as written in music. Music has the mystical power both to hold the player under its discipline so that one plays what the composer has set, while at the same time releasing the performer to interpret and play to the utmost limits of skill and inventiveness. Beginners have to stay strictly to the given music; the accomplished player interprets it with much more freedom. She looks and sees lurking within the score possibilities not written down. We are back to the character of play and game in the way we look at the world.

Is there something of a game going on between Jesus and that wonderful Canaanite woman (Matthew 15.21–8) in which her vision knocks up against convention? It is a fascinating encounter. She sees in the presence of Christ possibilities of healing for her daughter who 'is suffering terribly from demon-possession' (v. 22). A condition, we might think, which rules out any idea of game or playfulness as a horrible trivializing of the mother and daughter's desperation. But Jesus draws her out. He urges her to look at the present moment and imagine how it might be transformed. Does she see? Can she visualize possibilities for new life? He fends off her approach – 'Lord, Son of David, have mercy on me!' (v. 22) – by stating the accepted theological orthodoxy, 'I was sent only to the lost sheep of Israel' (v. 24).

The woman challenges the rules. Her vision demolishes the conventional readings. She attacks the Lord on his most vulnerable point (Is this a game? Chess? Football?), which is his compassion, with her heartbreaking cry, 'Lord, help me!' (v. 25). He counter-attacks and tries to catch her in his offside trap: 'It is not right to take the children's bread and toss it to their dogs' (v. 26 – this sounds like one of those antiphonal verbal war games still enjoyed in Islamic communities in the Far East. It can go on for ages!). But the woman has glimpsed healing for her daughter. She slips his offside ploy and advances to score the decisive goal with breathtaking audacity: 'Yes, Lord [...] but even the dogs eat the crumbs that fall from their masters' table' (v. 27). Game over. Jesus is totally won over by her vision which she pursued against all opposition, a marvellous instance of creative imagining (v. 28).

And the disciples? Those dull plods lost the plot at the outset of the encounter. All they could see were things obvious to anyone, a frantic foreigner who had no proper claim upon the Messiah making a nuisance of herself: 'Send her away, for she keeps crying out after us' (v. 23). A man writes about the death of a friend's five-year-old child of congenital heart failure, 'I realized in a profound way how fragile and yet how strong life is. I came face to face with the central power of God's mysterious presence and action in the world and in us. It is not by works that we are saved.' I include that note because, as we know too well, not all our children are healed as happily as the Canaanite girl. But even when faced with appalling loss the eye of faith is free to imagine with the imagination of our 'gloriously inventive artist of life' who brings life out of death.

Stay with this idea that the freedom to look which we have in Christ keeps taking on the form of a game. I am told that in the Russian Orthodox Easter Liturgy there comes a moment in the celebration of Christ's triumph over death and all its satellite powers, when at a signal from the priest the congregation burst into resurrection laughter. Laughter is the only possible response. Heaven rocks with that same laughter (see Revelation chapter 5), not because its people are comfortably untouched by events down here but because they see things as they are. 'Christ is risen!' is the decisive event and it is past, done, finished. Now view life from that vantage point. Resurrection has the last word, not death. We are in Christ free to look creatively, experimentally, into the troubled lives around us and see possibilities for resurrection.

If the outcome is already decided in Christ's resurrection, and yet we have to engage in the affairs of this life, then yes, our present existence has something of the game about it. It matters intensely that we give it our best shot, and yet the victory has already been won. Hans Urs von Balthasar connects the aspect of game with Jesus' choice of a child as the model for discipleship: 'Before you exert yourself, be aware that before God every exertion is but a game accepted in grace, a game that is not of itself important but that grace draws into the sphere of the important. Allow the tension of your efforts to be enfolded by the relaxed abandonment of a child's helpless faith.'[1]

Perhaps now we can see why the scriptures present our faith in such wonderfully upside-down, inside-out, wrong-way-round forms. Is this or is this not a great game which God invites us to enter and by which we are to look into the world with creative freedom? We read of a Lamb upon the throne; of a King who rides on a donkey to his enthronement on the cross; of the first who will be last; of people who though themselves paupers yet have powers 'to make many rich'. We read of those who find that 'when I am weak, then I am strong', and who die in order to live; of the meek who shall inherit the earth and 'a little child shall lead them'; of a death which kills death; and so we could go on. Does not this great paradox of reality as God sees it (which is the only real reality) dissolve our tramlines and our rigid ways of looking at life?

We are invited in our freedom to view the world with subversive, revolutionary sight, somewhat as a child in fact – a child delighting in things as seen for the first time. Viewed through this frankly anarchical inversion of the usual ordering of things – power, influence, importance, fame – after Christ had turned over the principalities and powers of the universe, laughter is our only possible response. George MacDonald wrote, 'It is the heart that is not yet sure of its God which is afraid to laugh in his presence.'[2]

Only the wonderfully inventive cosmic artist of light could have imagined the resurrection and in it the transfiguration of all things. The resurrection restores to us full joy in existence, the freedom to pass it through our imagination as we choose. Imagination is not fantasy but a movement towards reality. Coleridge felt that imagination is the most God-like aspect of any human being, a 'dim analogue of creation'.[3] It gives to each the Midas touch; to be constantly in possession of its transforming powers, for a visionary like Coleridge, meant life and joy and triumph. To lose it meant life slipping into somnambulism, a spiritual death.

We are saying that there is a will of God for every day of our lives but his will is always a release, never an inhibition. His will is to raise our own powers to maturity by allowing them full play. That is his marvellous design. In his poem 'The Destiny of Nations', Coleridge asked: 'For what is freedom, but the unfettered use of all the powers which God for use has given?' It is our selfishness, our rebellious egocentricity, which fetters our God-given powers, not his emancipating will. He calls us into a wonderful partnership by achieving his purposes through the choices we make and the work we fulfil, through the way we look at the world and dare to imagine life and blessing in barren places. We will conclude with an example out of the top drawer, Paul in Athens (Acts 17.16–34).

For the first time the Gospel was taken into the heartland of Greek culture. As usual Paul first visited the synagogue and 'reasoned [. . .] with the Jews and the God-fearing Greeks' (v. 17). He would have reasoned out of the Old Testament, in Jewish thought-forms, and stressing Christ as the fulfilment of prophecy. Next, we read, he went outside the synagogue and stepped into a different world: 'A group of Epicurean and Stoic philosophers began to dispute with him' (v. 18). Now he was playing away from home. We may assume Paul followed much the same line as he had with his Jewish audience earlier because the result was that the Athenians misheard, misunderstood, and misrepresented his message. We are especially interested in what happened next.

Remember, Paul came into Athens bathed in prayer, utterly dependent upon the Holy Spirit for power and guidance. God had his purposes for Athens and Paul's only concern was to play his part in furthering those purposes. But within that abandonment to the designs of God, Paul's intellectual and imaginative gifts move into top gear; fully trusting in the Spirit, fully free to imagine and to visualize a way forward.

In his imagination he projected on to that gathering of the Areopagus (the council which had supreme authority in religious matters) his uniquely personal vision of what could be done to exploit the situation for the kingdom of God.

This, now, is Paul in full flow. God released the man into full freedom, 'the unfettered use of all the powers which God for use had given', to visualize creatively what as yet did not exist (i.e. a meaningful and relevant explanation of Christ to sophisticated paganism). He had received and interpreted certain incoming signals when he toured the city. Now his imagination selected one and saw in it a powerful way into the Athenian mind. God trusted the man to do this creative work; Paul could have come at it in other ways but he courageously chose to take his text not from the Bible but from the very heart of Athenianism: '[. . .] as I walked around and looked carefully at your objects of worship, I even found an altar with this inscription: TO AN UNKNOWN GOD' (v. 23).

Paul heard in that altar inscription the cry for help out of the heart of Greek culture. From that way in (and he had their attention immediately) he projected forward his argument, using their own poets as stepping stones towards Christ.

We say again, in the purposes of God we discover the fullest freedom of all our powers and gifts. God trusts us to demonstrate how 'wisdom is proved right by all her children' (Luke 7.35). Children of the 'gloriously inventive artist of light' will delight in their freedom to look and listen inventively.

CHAPTER 14

Beyond custom

ɞc ɞc ɞc

Raise a glass to the most underrated of all great little beasts, Balaam's ass, who gave his rider the lesson of a lifetime. The famed seer-magician could not see what was as plain as day to his donkey – an angel of the Lord in the road ahead. But then, Balaam was always a devious and self-absorbed man (Numbers 22.21–3 l).

On the other hand, Jesus' disciples were on the whole no more devious or self-absorbed than the rest of us (with one well-known exception). They simply could not 'see' those children or 'hear' what was going on with that Canaanite woman mentioned in the previous chapter. It was too easy for us to mock their dimness. Is it reasonable to blame someone for failing to see what they cannot see? That triggers the next question, and it is an alarming one for those who aspire to some participation in God's mission: how could followers who shared so intimately and intensely in Christ's ministry remain so dull for so long?

It is easier to spot spiritual ineptitude in others than in ourselves, especially when viewed from a distance. We can detect in the disciples the usual conditioning effect of custom, tradition, bias, and the accepted orthodoxies of the day. We each have them and we are shaped by them. We can no more escape their influence than we can jump away from our own shadow. Attitudes of which the individual is hardly aware (until she travels a bit) have powers to refract and distort her perceptions and to filter out from incoming messages those aspects which do not agree with her 'normal' patterns of understanding.

In their defence you may point out that the disciples had not at that time received the Holy Spirit. Their minds and imaginations, sight and hearing, were not yet under the quickening illumination of the indwelling Spirit of revelation. Then consider what happened following Pentecost. In Acts we are given a disturbing account of a Spirit-baptized community which emerged with certain decisive pre-Pentecost and very Jewish attitudes untouched.

The Jerusalem church, in spite of the activity of the Holy Spirit, still viewed the world and interpreted the Gospel through the filters of their Judaistic traditions. They insisted on gentile converts conforming to a Judaistic form of Christianity. Even Peter succumbed to the pressure of the culture and traditions. Paul on the other hand saw only too well what was going on and would have none of it (Acts 15). That struggle was the first major threat to the existence of the young church, much more dangerous and life-threatening than brutal persecutions.

We would never have found Paul evangelizing in Athens with such brilliant and creative freedom, proclaiming Christ via a pagan altar inscription, had he toed the Jewish line of the mother church in Jerusalem. As it was he moved away, and went up to Antioch where his church became the dynamic centre of missionary expansion throughout the Mediterranean world. Meanwhile the Jerusalem church, blinkered by her customs and traditions, disappeared from the record, never heard of again in the New Testament except as a community in urgent need of financial support from Paul's churches (Romans 15.25–6).

Peter, eventually, was jolted out of his prejudices by the vision of ceremonially impure and unclean creatures *coming down out of heaven*. His instinct was ludicrously to imply that God had a debased view of the Gospel and creation, that God had forgotten his own scriptures and really ought to be more Jewish! Then Peter saw: all people stand on level ground within the love of God. Any traditions which dilute or block that understanding must be rejected root and branch (Acts 10.9–23).

We have our own traditions: venerable or recent, complex and structured or open and free-falling. We, too, may discover (if we can find a way of standing outside of them for awhile) that we cannot hear or see the world for the noise and distractions of those traditions. In which case we will never appreciate the context in which our church members live and in which the church is set as witness. How can we respond to what we cannot hear or see? Further, if, as we believe, the Lord is in the heart of the world and speaks through its hunger, we are trapped in a bizarre situation: Christ's incoming word to us is drowned out by the attitudes of Christ's church. Bizarre, but horribly familiar. Our mission is then shunted into a churchy cul-de-sac where we pass our time in morale-boosting events, a threat to no one.

Here is a tremendous question for every Christian and each congregation: how is it that traditions whose original purpose were to bring us closer to God and his mission may metamorphose into their opposite? They may actually render us insensitive to God's word as it comes to us from all directions out of his world. And having traced the deathly tendency back to its source, can it be reversed and we become attuned to the God who speaks and acts?

Before we get deeper into this, and to save us from despair of ever escaping our self-binding traditions, we will name the redeeming, transforming answer – the attitude, or gift, or quality, which can give new birth to those ambiguous traditions of ours, both personal and ecclesiastical. We speak of love. Therefore, in the heart of his greatest teaching on the spiritual gifts whereby we can hear God and see his activity, Paul placed his profound words on love (1 Corinthians 13). A Christian community like that at Corinth, breathing the air of Greek gnosticism with its thirst for more and more esoteric knowledge, is called to the pursuit of love.

All gifts, any gifts, including wealth, are safe in the hands of people who love. Do you seriously desire to see and hear God in his world? But you suspect that your received attitudes, customs and cultural conditioning, not to mention your bias, pride, and vanity, could be screening you off from what God is trying to communicate to you? Then seek what Paul calls 'the more excellent way' (1 Corinthians 12.31, AV). Wash your inner life in love and you will be saved. We cannot do better than meditate on Paul's teaching and notice how love makes wise lookers and listeners of us all. What is someone leading an authentic, creative life really like? The answer is simply that person is one who loves.

First, for all that he says about love, Paul nowhere defines it. There is a knowledge which descends to the heart. Only people who love, who have experienced it, understand its essence. Above all, love has to be tasted and experienced, not defined. Paul does give demarcations – he says that love looks like this, never like that – but no definition in a dictionary sense.

1 'If I speak in the tongues of men and of angels, but have not love, I am only a resounding gong or a clanging cymbal.'
2 'If I have the gift of prophecy and can fathom all mysteries and all knowledge, and if I have faith that can move mountains, but have not love, I am nothing.'
3 'If I give all I possess to the poor and surrender my body to the flames, but have not love, I gain nothing.'

Or as we might say, in terms of our own exploration, 'If I have the most penetrating sight and perceptive hearing but have not love, I am nothing.'

This is very surprising because clearly the wondrous qualities of speech; knowledge and prophecy; and self-sacrifice in verses 1–3 are very much something. But not from where God is standing, which at the end of the day is the only perspective which matters. Love, apparently, is when I place myself into what I do for the sake of other people. Unless I am in those acts (speech, knowledge, interpretation, sacrifice), they are empty. Superficially impressive, but declared by God to be empty. Then why do things at all? Probably for egocentric reasons and in order to impress other people.

Love has substantial ways of looking and listening which are experienced and not merely performed: more like the observation of a lover than that of a sociologist; more like a brother than an academic. A way of looking at people around me which has meaning and content because I am committed to those I observe. Paul is saying that above all else love is concern and service for others. As Christians we must ask if we have the right to look and listen for God in the affairs of the world unless it is with the desire to serve.

There is a gathering of news about the world done in order to make a stick to beat the world. A desire to be up on social trends, to be able to talk interestingly about 'modernity' or even 'post-modernity' but at heart motivated by a contempt for a society which will not believe our message or come to our services. Paul insists that it all amounts to nothing, a well-shaped emptiness, unless we are ourselves in it for the sake of others.

Even at this early stage in Paul's teaching we can see how our most deeply ingrained attitudes are dragged out into the light by the power of love. Each custom, tradition, personal as well as congregational habit of mind, must give an account of itself in the presence of love. The spiritual writer Ladislaus Boros says:

> First prove that you value the other person more than your own life and that you will defend him from the cares of the world and the injuries it can inflict. Give him shelter. Protect him, if necessary, against himself. Fight for him, give him life, let him grow and expand inwardly. Talking about love is, for Paul, empty and hollow without the experience and action of love.[1]

Looking and listening are the essential servants of love. They do love's bidding. They scan the surrounding world in order to express love in self-effacing service for others. Traditions go into the melting-pot of love. Love teaches me that what has real value are not formulations of words, however true or impressive, moving or profound, but self-surrender. Imagine the difference it would make to the quality and impact of our lives if our first tradition was self-surrender. It is, after all, the first tradition in the Godhead, where Father, Son and Spirit each pour themselves out to the other in utter self-surrender. God is love.

But what of Paul's words that even the utter extremes of self-sacrifice (possessions to the poor, body to the flames) amount to nothing without love? This is a staggering claim but maybe not so staggering when we test it against our own hearts. 'Acts of love' may not be motivated by love but desire for self-fulfilment; self-justification; to appear unusual; a show of love for others and for God which in fact is self-obsessed. We are so convoluted in our motivations and desires that our acts of love can be done without love and are therefore deemed empty, meaningless. Indeed they may even be directed *against* people. There is an essential selflessness about love.

Yet there is such a thing as a proper self-regard, a self-love. God has given to each of us a unique, distinctive self. Everything is gift. We are quick to tell people how they ought to receive God's gifts with gratitude and handle them with due care and reverence. The first and greatest gift you have received is the gift of your own being, your self and existence – an astonishing gift which is able to receive the second gift, of God's own self. The self you received is what it is in order to be able to receive the self of God. Just as we would honour and tend a place of worship as the house of God, for the same reasons but raised to a vastly greater power, you should love yourself. Tend, honour, cultivate it.

But at the same time, and along with the truth of self-love, love calls us to selflessness, even to a kind of self-forgetfulness. Without it, even supreme acts of sacrifice amount to nothing.

Self-forgetfulness is a not-knowing-about oneself. In fact we find ourselves continuously tuned in to the demands made by those selves on ourselves. For all the talk of free will we are in fact enslaved to the stream of demands sent up from the self. But love is quite simply serving others without ourselves' ulterior motives and agendas. It is service for the real good of the other person and wanting nothing in return. It suggests a person who 'lives away from' the self, who moves the centre of gravity of his being outside himself.

Those are insights which have the effect of leaving us shattered by the inescapable, revolutionary presence of love. But there follows from Paul an extraordinarily homely and down-to-earth description of love's attitudes in the most practical terms.

4 Love is patient, love is kind. It does not envy, it does not boast, it is not proud.

5 It is not rude, it is not self-seeking, it is not easily angered, it keeps no record of wrongs.

6 Love does not delight in evil but rejoices with the truth.

7 It always protects, always trusts, always hopes, always perseveres.

8 Love never fails (i.e. it will never come to an end).

There is no need for us to go phrase by phrase through Paul's words. Rather, add them up and state the total. What do they amount to, particularly as they affect our habits of looking and listening which are themselves governed by our attitudes of mind and our traditions?

In total, love is described as our selfless efforts to bear with people, to sustain them in their needs, and to help them bear their own lives. It suggests the commitment and courage to hang on for people, faithfully and with patience. The person who loves like this is reliable and consistent, not as a doormat but in order to open up a future for the other person. The loving person does what she can to make life liveable and bearable for others, to allow others space and encouragement to flourish.

Therefore such a person keeps herself, her intrusive, clamouring, vain and touchy self, under control. We conclude that such a person has a distinctive quality and power in the way she looks and listens to the world. The rubbish acquired by the self-absorbed is cleared out of the way. This person is profoundly free and unbiased to see and hear things as they are and what God is saying in the world. From Paul's astonishing text, we take in particular this description of love: 'Love does not delight in evil but rejoices in the truth.' We look into the world not to condemn it or to despair of it, from the safety of our churches, but to weep at the evil, to rejoice at the truth and to participate in God's saving and transforming mission in the world.

We are discovering that the art of true looking and hearing consists first in becoming a certain kind of person inspired by love. Indeed, the principle seems to be: love, and let the looking and listening take care of itself.

A delightful application of that principle is found in Newman's comment on how a Christian should behave towards others. It smacks of another age but is even more striking for it. He calls his Christian 'the gentleman':

He is one who never inflicts pain [. . .] he is mainly occupied in merely removing the obstacles which hinder the free and unembarrassed action of those about him [. . .] he is like an easy chair or a good fire [. . .] he carefully avoids whatever may cause a jar or a jolt in the minds of those with whom he is cast [. . .] his great concern being to make everyone at their ease and at home [. . .] he is tender towards the bashful, gentle towards the distant, and merciful towards the absurd [. . .] he is seldom prominent in conversation and never wearisome. He makes light of favours while he does them, and seems to be receiving when

he is conferring [. . .] [he believes] that we should ever
conduct ourselves towards our enemy as if he were one day
to be our friend [. . .] he is as simple as he is forcible, and
as brief as he is decisive. Nowhere shall we find greater
candour, consideration, indulgence: he throws himself into
the minds of his opponents, he accounts for their mistakes
[. . .][2]

The impression conveyed of the person, the 'gentleman', in
Newman's sketch is of someone essentially at peace with
himself, free enough from the tyranny of his own self to be
available to others, positively looking out for the well-being
and the sensitivity of others to such an extent that it sounds to
us now almost quaint. In fact it is a beautiful incarnation of
Paul's love teaching, showing a person not rendered short-
sighted or partially deaf by his own tradition-system, but
rejoicing in the truth of others.

So much for our detour to visit love, 'the singing master of
the soul' and the source of Christ-like looking and listening;
love, which has mystical powers to transform bigots into open
and generous-minded people, and to dissolve our inflexible
patterns of custom and of cultural conditioning. With this
answer in mind, we can proceed with our inquiry into the way
God speaks out of the life of the world.

CHAPTER 15

Hearing a new voice

ꗃ ꗃ ꗃ

We have our model, our ideal and prototype, in the Lord Jesus Christ: what was good enough for Jesus will be good enough for us. He revealed that it is the hearing, the hearing above all, that makes a human being. That and the corresponding gift of speech, the being able to answer. Jesus lived out the picture prophesied of him by Isaiah:

> The Sovereign Lord has given me an instructed tongue,
>> to know the word that sustains the weary.
> He wakens me morning by morning,
>> wakens my ear to listen like one being taught.
> The Sovereign Lord has opened my ears,
>> and I have not been rebellious;
>> I have not drawn back.
>
> (Isaiah 50.4–5)

The servant of the Lord faces out towards the nations, he is a world personality. Jerusalem is his city,

> 'and all nations will stream to it'.
> Many peoples will come and say,
> 'Come, let us go up to the mountain of the Lord [. . .]'
> (Isaiah 2.2–3)

The servant of the Lord has a global strategy: 'In that day there will be a highway from Egypt to Assyria. The Assyrians will go to Egypt and the Egyptians to Assyria' – not for purposes of war but for another astonishing reason: 'The Egyptians and Assyrians will worship together.'

There follows an even more incredible prediction concerning ancient enemies: 'In that day Israel will be third, along with Egypt and Assyria, a blessing on the earth. The Lord Almighty will bless them, saying, "Blessed be Egypt my people, Assyria my handiwork, and Israel my inheritance"' (Isaiah 19.23–5)

The servant of the Lord is a cosmic figure: his business is with the nations, he trades with every culture and with all the peoples of the earth. He has his ear to the heart of the world. It follows that his people who are conforming to his image will listen for their Lord's voice coming out of the affairs of the world.

We remember that the one we here call the 'servant of the Lord' is also 'Wisdom' who 'calls aloud in the street, she raises her voice in the public squares; at the head of the noisy streets she cries out, in the gateways of the city she makes her speech' (Proverbs 1.20–1). The Lord is in the thick of the action where the crowds gather. His people look and listen for him. Or do they? Allow me a last personal experience.

We were travelling by train to Edinburgh. Across the gangway from our seat was a group of four rather tough-looking young men. Every few minutes they would huddle together in deep conversation, then write something down in a notebook. Were they up to no good, we wondered, perhaps planning some mischief among the unsuspecting citizens of Edinburgh? As I said, they had the appearance of rather intimidating toughness. Then quite suddenly one of them looked up, caught my wife looking at him and gave her a terrific smile. It was getting interesting. Then from out of one of the group's whispering huddles I picked up some startling words '. . . Jesus . . . prayer . . . Bible . . . the Holy Spirit . . .'.

Unable to bear it any longer I leaned over and accused them of being Christians. Indeed they were, young in the faith, and full of it. 'There are twenty of us in the train – we are going up to Scotland for a conference of our congregations. You see him over there?' – they said, pointing to an older man – 'He's our pastor. He's just done twenty years in prison.' In fact everyone in their group had come to faith either in prison or during drug rehabilitation, or both. I wanted to know about their churches. Their explanation left me feeling embarrassed, ashamed and angry.

They told me that when they came out of prison, or drug rehab, with their new faith in Christ they did as their spiritual counsellors advised and sought out various local churches. It appears that those congregations were either unable or unwilling to receive these new converts and provide support and relevant forms of fellowship and learning. I do not for a second underestimate the difficulties, for both sides, when young men fresh out of prison try to integrate with a congregation of people with more 'normal' life-styles. Eventually my friends on the train, and hundreds more around the country, gave up on the 'normal' churches and formed their own fellowships, small congregations of tremendous energy and Christian realism. But consider what influx of new life, what experiences of the Lord's forgiveness, what testimony to the saving power of the Gospel, those regular churches let go!

Surely God speaks out of the dark experiences of people in prison or oppressed by addiction. Those young men, I felt, carried a word of hope, of new possibilities, of lives transformed in a radical, primitive and most practical faith. A word we in the 'regular' churches urgently need to hear – but, if my friends' experiences are typical, it is a word falling on deaf ears. 'Wisdom' calls out of the unhappiness of damaged lives but, somehow, we are not attuned to her voice. I suggest those young men in the Edinburgh train carry a prophetic word of power and contemporary relevance seldom encountered in our churches.

One church-watcher observes that churches can change from being a movement to being a machine and from being a machine to being a monument. Writing out of her experience of young churches in the Philippines, Melba Maggay comments:

[T]he early stage where a movement generated excitement because its ideas are fresh, its leadership charismatic, and its mission sharp and clear, soon gives way to a stage where things become more efficient and routinised: Charisma is ritualised, purpose becomes platform, and conviction is systematised into a creed. If this continues and no fresh element reforms or reshapes the institution it hardens and petrifies into a monument, a sad relic of days gone by when the Spirit blew and blasted to bits sacrosanct ways of doing things.[1]

As metaphors of the life of a church, 'machines, monuments and institutions' are not able to discern the directions and trends of the kingdom of God in the world. Not without much creaking, painful upheaval and honest self-examination. It does not follow that our traditions necessarily affect us negatively, simply that they may filter out the prophetic word of God.

The Latin American theologian, Gustavo Gutiérrez, points out that Christians in his part of the world discovered the social dimension of their faith without abandoning their Christ-centred spirituality. The renowned Archbishop Romero, for one example, remained very much a traditional churchman when exercising his courageous protest against the sufferings and oppression of the people of El Salvador. His attachment to his tradition did not prevent him from direct contact with the poor. He heard the voice of the Lord in the cries of the people.

Jesus told a parable to illustrate one attitude which renders a church effectively blind and deaf to the needs of its surrounding world: the parable of the workers in the vineyard (Matthew 21.33–43). Any congregation could very usefully take this parable as a means of doing the elusive and difficult thing, and scrutinizing its obedience to the Lord.

In that parable the owner who planted and established the vineyard installed a group of workers to care for it and manage the produce in his absence. But notice the change in the workers' relationship to the vineyard and the owner. In his absence they increasingly saw themselves not as employees but as owners. From being workers in it, they became, in their own understanding, controllers over it. From serving the needs of the vineyard, the vineyard increasingly served their needs to the extent that they rejected a succession of agents sent by the owner. Finally, they murdered the owner's son in order to clinch their claim to the vineyard.

The questions for every church to consider are: who owns the vineyard? For whom and for what purpose does the vineyard (the kingdom of God and, within the kingdom, the Church) exist?

It is difficult not to conclude that the churches (and surely they were typical of the majority) to which the young men on the train had turned, and met apathy or bewilderment or even hostility, had taken control of the purposes of the vineyard. What had emerged were church programmes to suit the needs and interests of the resident congregation. And why not? They run the place and are committed to its survival and future. But again we come back to our Lord's story: for whom does the vineyard-church exist? For the purposes of the owner who is out seeking people in his world.

Once we lose sight of that absolutely fundamental truth, we inevitably and inexorably fall deaf and blind towards what the world is trying to say to us. For all the appearances of our piety and orthodoxies we have effectively ejected the rightful owner and seized control for ourselves. Not instantaneously or dramatically of course, and not deliberately, but as a steady drift and in ways described by Melba Maggay.

Then life in the vineyard of the church degenerates into a self-regarding and self-perpetuating affair (like a machine in fact, and some machines are very impressive), ordered to the approval of its clientele. Then only those strategies which suit the interests of the renegade workers-turned-owners are allowed a place. Therefore things such as times of services, styles of worship and learning, the language used, the patterns of outreach, are arranged to reflect the inner-group. The Bible, if given serious attention at all, is heard through those filters and few even raise the possibility that there could be a word from God seeking a hearing and acceptance in the church. A word arriving in the form, say, of a young Christian just out of prison. Any such divine word is drowned out by the whirring and grinding of the church machine.

God plants the vineyard for the sake of the world, not for the pleasure of its members. Therefore a church can only fulfil its calling by sustaining and developing conversations with its world. Of course the key to a vital conversation lies with the average church member who, presumably, lives in the local world. Congregations are made up of many lizards and a few frogs. Maybe one frog. How do frogs hunt for their food? The answer is they don't; instead, they wait for a bug or a fly to come close and snap it up. Clergy, full-time ministers, are like frogs. Their job is to stay pretty much in the centre of the life of their congregation and respond to people as they approach.

Lizards, on the other hand, forage for their food. That is the congregation who are out and about on their business from Monday to Friday. How very odd, then, that it is the clergy who interpret to their congregations the needs and the interests of the local world. But in the nature of their work, ministers during the day are involved mostly with the elderly, the infirm, and 'mums and toddlers' – type groups. Meanwhile the lizards are out in the tough world earning their living.

Frogs are important to an effective church. And it is as mistaken to want frogs to become lizards as it is to expect exhausted lizards to rush home and turn into frogs for the evening or the weekend. Both are essential and need each other. My point is this: the people who have most hope of discerning what God is saying in and through the world are the lizards. Frogs (and I speak as one) are inclined to put a theoretical, bookish, second-hand, arms-length slant on news coming in from the outside world. And if you say that the lizards in your own congregation display no lively interest in decoding their Monday-to-Friday world, perhaps that is because it is not their tradition, or the tradition of your church, to encourage them in it. I heard the comment recently that 'the job of the laity in the church is to pay and to pray'. Splendid things to do, but what of the way they read their world? By all means let frogs be frogs, and lizards be lizards, but let us hear more from the lizards.

The vineyard, which is the church in the kingdom of God exists for the sake of the world as a demonstration of what life under God's love is like. Therefore, notice the sting in the tail of Christ's parable. What a sting it is! The owner will not tolerate the unlawful seizure of his vineyard (Matthew 21.40–1). He comes down upon those who misuse it and attempt to divert its life toward their own ends. 'Therefore I tell you that the kingdom of God will be taken away from you and given to a nation who will produce its proper fruit' (v. 43).

First, taken away from an unbelieving Israel and given to the Gentiles. But with the same solemn warning from the owner of the vineyard: tend it, develop it, keep it on behalf of the nations, keep the doors open to whosoever may want to come in and taste the fruit. Remember! No superiority; no class, race, life-style distinctions; no misuse or exploitation of the vineyard, no redirecting it towards your own interests. Hold it for the world. And remember, what happened to Israel can also happen to you (Romans 11.17–24). Listen for the owner, attend to his directives, look out for his agents, stay awake, fulfil your calling.

We conclude therefore that only as a church is on the move, within the purposes of God (which is not the same as merely being busy and active), will it be an authentic, listening community open to the owner's world. For such a church, looking and listening are a life-necessity. Only a moving church will feel its urgent dependence upon God for guidance and power. Only a church on the move will realize that its traditions, however rich and venerable, cannot deliver God's new word for its future. It will have proper respect for its traditions and customary way of doing things yet keep them where they work best, under the illumination of the owner's prophetic word.

If a church is not on the move, if it is not in its essence a movement, it can only be one other thing, an institution. To help you scrutinize the status of your own church, as movement or institution, here is a simple check-list which compares and contrasts the characteristics of each:

- An institution is by its nature conservative.
  A movement is progressive.
- An institution-church tends to leave everything calm, balanced, pleasing to the majority.
  A movement-church leaves a trail of wonder and delight but also (probably) disturbance and resentment.
- An institution-church is passive, yielding to influences from outside, reactionary.
  A movement-church is active, influencing rather than being influenced, an initiator, creative, an imaginative innovator.
- An institution-church looks to its past.
  A movement-church looks to the future.
- The institutional mind is cautious, anxious, aware of itself and its history, touchy about its status, defensive.
  The movement-mind takes risks, it is not much concerned for its reputation.
- An institution-church guards its boundaries.
  The movement-church is by instinct always looking to cross boundaries.
- The institution-church suspects that the Gospel does not travel easily or translate into other cultures or life-styles.

> *The movement people are convinced that the Gospel is incorrigibly nomadic!*

- An institution-church does not, as an instinct, stand open before the surrounding world attuned to whatever God is choosing to say. It becomes, therefore, inevitably a 'community of predictability'.

> *The movement-church assumes that the Lord is active in the affairs of society and seeks to discern the divine voice however expressed and from whatever point of the compass. It is therefore a 'community of possibility'.*

We saw earlier how two churches, the one at Jerusalem and the other at Antioch, epitomized the struggle between the movement and the institutional mentalities.

Finally, perhaps we can restate that struggle as listening for God's 'old voice'. and his 'new voice'. In this our personal and individual spirituality is involved as much as our congregations'; the way you look to God for direction, as much as the way your church seeks its guidance. We turn to that strange event involving Elijah, a man at the end of his tether and desperately in need of a fresh encounter with God (I Kings 19).

Elijah had spent his energies vindicating God before the massed prophets of Baal on Carmel. There followed classic post-mission burn-out: exhaustion, depression, terrible loss of confidence and fear, taking him to the edge of suicide (v. 4). God responds with food and sleep, followed by more food and sleep until Elijah was able to get himself together and seek fresh commissioning for the next move in his prophetic ministry. For that, he knew exactly where to go: to Horeb, 'the mountain of God', the holy place of theophanies where Moses, also at his wits' end, had met God in the burning bush.

Furthermore, Elijah knew how the Lord would reveal himself in that encounter: he would appear, as he always did to his servants at crucial times, in the classic signs and wonders, in convulsions in nature – wind, fire, earth tremors – the divine calling-card.

God gave Elijah his signs in an awesome display. But Elijah found that the Lord was not in 'the wind [. . .] the earthquake [. . .] the fire' (vv. 11–12). That is to say, Elijah searched for the word of God along his traditional lines but found them silent. A strange thing had happened to Elijah: his assumptions, based on his past experience, that God comes in signs of power were *dis*confirmed by a great display of power! Wind, earthquake and fire were found to contain nothing but wind, earthquake and fire. God's 'old' way of speaking had fallen silent.

As we often find, in times of crisis and personal despair, our well-tried ways of hearing God may produce nothing. Perhaps that is why he allows us to pass through such times. For Elijah at that moment God spoke in his 'new' voice and it is to Elijah's enormous credit that he was still there, waiting, looking, listening for however God would speak to him.

'And after the fire came a gentle whisper' (v. 12) – so translates the New International Version. Other modern translations give a similar form of words. Each explains what Elijah heard, in terms we can manage. But in so doing they have completely demystified the text. The Hebrew is haunting, strange, other-worldly, and untranslatable: it describes God's 'new' voice at that moment as 'a voice of thin silence' (whatever does that mean?) or 'a small voice of silence' (equally elusive). But there is nothing mysterious or unusual about 'a gentle whisper'. The REB gives 'a faint murmuring sound', which reminds me of the noise our bedroom radiator makes when the central heating comes on. Hardly a sound which suggests strange otherness. The AV's 'still small voice' comes closest.

Or else the translation suggested by Rabbi Lawrence Kushner, that Elijah heard 'the soft barely audible sound of almost breathing'.[2] That suggests that the 'new' voice of God was as close, as internal, as soft as Elijah's own breathing; God speaking not only 'out there' in great displays of power, but also 'in here' as near as the thoughts arising in our mind and imagination. The New Testament agrees when it refers to the Holy Spirit as 'the Spirit of wisdom and revelation' who arises in the believer so that 'the eyes of your heart may be enlightened' (Ephesians 1.17, 18); the Spirit of God by whom 'we have the mind of Christ' (1 Corinthians 2.16).

An inner whisper, barely audible, but a decisive word of God; for what Elijah heard lifted him out of despair and sent him back north again to organize a double *coup d'état* in Syria and Israel. By that 'soft barely audible sound of almost breathing' God continues to direct the nations.

References

❧❧❧

CHAPTER 1 Beyond the web

1 *The New York Times*, 7 July 1957, quoted in Marshall McLuhan, *Understanding Media*, Routledge and Kegan Paul, London, 1964.
2 Marcel, G. *The Mystery of Being*, quoted in John O'Donnell SJ, *Hans Urs von Balthasar*, Geoffrey Chapman, London, 1992, p. 73.

CHAPTER 2 Facing out

1 'The Face of God' (3rd–4th cent. AD), from T. Carmi, ed., *The Penguin Book of Hebrew Verse*, Penguin, Harmondsworth, 1981, p. 196.
2 Farrer, A., *The End of Man*, SPCK, London, 1973, p. 4.

CHAPTER 4 Slow looking

1 Farrer, A., *Reflective Faith*, SPCK, London, 1972, pp. 37, 38.
2 von Balthasar, H. U., *Does Jesus Know Us? Do We Know Him?*, Ignatius Press, San Francisco, 1983, p. 26.

CHAPTER 5 Expect to see owls

1 Warren, E., 'Christographia XIV', in Thomas Howard, ed., *Chance or the Dance?*, Ignatius Press, San Francisco, 1992.
2 From 'Pied Beauty', in *The Poems of Gerard Manley Hopkins*, Oxford University Press, Oxford, 1967.
3 Quoted in *The Independent* Magazine, 7 May 1994.
4 From 'The Destiny of Nations', in *Selected Poems of Samuel Taylor Coleridge*, Oxford University Press, Oxford, 1967.
5 von Balthasar, H. U., 'The Grain of Wheat', in *Aphorisms*, Ignatius Press, San Francisco, 1995, p. 127.

6 'The Elixir', in *George Herbert: The Complete English Poems*, Penguin, Harmondsworth, 1991.

CHAPTER 6 Before talk

1 Quoted in Knight, G. A. F., *Psalms, Daily Bible Study*, vol.1, Saint Andrew Press, Edinburgh, 1982.
2 Quoted in Ulanov, A. and B., *Primary Speech: a psychology of prayer*, SCM. London, 1982.
3 See Knight, George A. F., *A Christian Theology of the Old Testament*, SCM, London, 1959, pp. 111–13.
4 von Balthasar, H. U., quoted in O'Donnell *Hans Urs von Balthasar*, p. 72.

CHAPTER 9 Imagination overawed

1 House, H. and Storey, G. (eds), *The Journals and Papers of Gerard Manley Hopkins*, quoted in Martin, R. B., *Gerard Manley Hopkins: A Very Private Life*, Flamingo, London, 1992, p. 203.
2 Hopkins, G. M., *Poems and Prose*, selected by W. H. Gardner, Penguin, Harmondsworth, 1988, p. 120.
3 Traherne, T., *Centuries*, The Faith Press, London, 1960, 1:28.
4 Kushner, L., *The Book of Words*, Jewish Lights Publishing, Woodstock, Vermont, 1993, pp. 19, 20.

CHAPTER 10 Listening for God

1 Peterson, E., 'Contemplative Exegesis', *The Reformed Journal* (USA), May 1987.
2 Quoted in Heaney, S., *The Redress of Poetry*, Faber, London, 1995, p. 1.
3 Steiner, G., *Real Presences*, Faber, London, 1989, p. 9.

CHAPTER 11 Different readings

1 Yeats, W. B., 'Sailing to Byzantium', in Tim Webb, ed., *Selected Poetry*, Penguin, Harmondsworth, 1991.
2 Mackenzie, N. H., *A Reader's Guide to Gerard Manley Hopkins*, Thames and Hudson, London, 1981, p. 233.

3 Hopkins, *Poems and Prose*, p. 127.
4 Hopkins, *Poems and Prose*, p. 124.
5 Hopkins, *Poems and Prose*, p. 125.

CHAPTER 12 Memory-sight

1 Rose, S., *The Making of Memory*, Bantam Books, London, 1993, p. 1.

CHAPTER 13 Look as you will

1 von Balthasar, H. U., 'The Grain of Wheat', p. 43.
2 Lewis, C. S., (ed.) *Georqe MacDonald: An Anthology*, Geoffrey Bles, London, 1946.
3 Quoted in Willey, B., *Nineteenth Century Studies*, Chatto and Windus, London, 1950, p. 14.

CHAPTER 14 Beyond custom

1 Boros, L., *Meditations*, Search Press, London, 1974, p. 43.
2 Newman, J. H., Quoted in *A Newman Treasury*, C. F. Harrold, ed., Arlington House, New Rochelle, New York, 1975, p. 272.

CHAPTER 15 Hearing a new voice

1 Maggay, M., *Transforming Society*, Regnum Lynx, Oxford, 1994, p. 88.
2 Kushner, L., *The Book of Words*, p. 27.